Thomas
Cook

HOTSPOTS
MALLORCA

G000150914

Written and researched by Tony Kelly, updated by Teresa Fisher
Front cover photography courtesy of Thomas Cook Tour Operations Ltd

Original design concept by Studio 183 Limited
Series design by Bridgewater Books
Cover design/artwork by Lee Biggadike, Studio 183 Limited

Produced by the Bridgewater Book Company
The Old Candlemakers, West Street, Lewes, East Sussex BN7 2NZ, United Kingdom
www.bridgewaterbooks.co.uk
Project Editor: Emily Casey Bailey
Project Designer: Lisa McCormick

Published by Thomas Cook Publishing
A division of Thomas Cook Tour Operations Limited
PO Box 227, Units 15-16, Coningsby Road, Peterborough PE3 8SB, United Kingdom
email: books@thomascook.com
www.thomascookpublishing.com
+ 44 (0) 1733 416477

ISBN-13: 978-1-84157-537-7
ISBN-10: 1-84157-537-2

Head of Thomas Cook Publishing: Chris Young
Project Editor: Diane Ashmore
Production/DTP Editor: Steven Collins

Printed and bound in Spain by Graficas Cems, Navarra, Spain

CONTENTS

SYMBOLS KEY

The following is a key to the symbols used throughout this book:

information office	post office	restaurant
bus stop	airport	café
church	tip	bar
train station	shopping	fine dining

t telephone f fax e email w website address

a address opening times important

€ budget price €€ mid-range price €€€ most expensive

★ special interest ★★ see if passing ★★★ top attraction

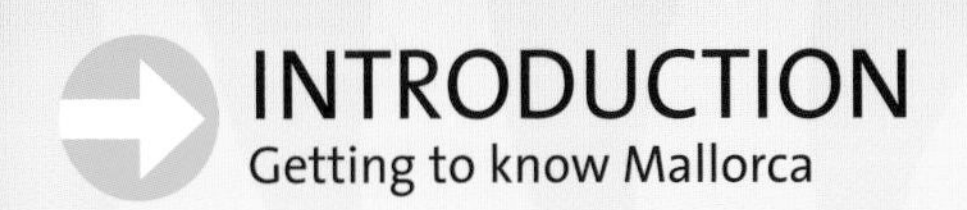

INTRODUCTION
Getting to know Mallorca

Bay of Biscay
FRANCE
Atlantic Ocean
PORTUGAL
SPAIN
MALLORCA
Mediterranean Sea
MOROCCO
ALGERIA
TORRENT DE PAREIS
PUIG MAJOR
PORT DE SÓLLER
FOMALUTX
SÓLLER
DEIA
SERRA DE TRAMUNTANA
Castell
VALLDEMOSSA
BANYALBUFAR
BUNYOLA
ALARÓ
BINISSALEM
ESPORLES
Sa Granja
PALMANYOLA
CONSELL
ESTELLENCS
SANTA MARIA DEL CAMÍ
SA CABANETA
SANTA EUGENIA
PÒRTOL
SANT ELM
ANDRATX
S'ARRACÓ
CALVIÁ
SANT AGUSTI
PALMA
COLL DEN RABASSA
CALA MAJOR
ILLETES
PORTALS NOUS
PORT D'ANDRATX
PEGUERA
CA'N PASTILLA
PLAYA DE PALMA
S'ARENAL
SANTA PONÇA
PALMA NOVA
MAGALUF / TORRENOVA
CALA VINYES
Cap de Cala Figuera
BADIA GRAN
CAPOCORB VELL
Cap Blanc
N
0
10
20 km
0
6
12 miles

Cap de Formentor
CASTEL DEL REI
CALA SANT VICENÇ
PORT DE POLLENÇA
POLLENÇA
ALCÚDIA
PORT D'ALCÚDIA
Roman Theatre
Bahia de Alcúdia
CAMPANET
SA POBLA
MOSCARI
BUGER
CA'N PICAFORT
MURO
SERRA NOVA
SA COLÒNIA DE SANT PERE
CALA RAJADA
SANTA MARGALIDA
LLUBI
CAPDEPERA
ARTÀ
MARIA DE LA SALUT
COSTITX
SINEU
ARIANY
SA COSTA DES PINS
SON SERVERA
LLORET DE VISTA ALEGRE
PETRA
SANT LLORENÇ DES CARDASSAR
CALA BONA
SANT JOAN
CALA MILLOR
SA COMA
MONTUÏRI
VILLAFRANCA DE BONANY
MANACOR
S'ILLOT
PORTO CRISTO
Coves del Drac
CALA ROMANTICA
PORRERES
FELANITX
CALES DE MALLORCA
CALA MURADA
CAMPOS
PORTO COLOM / CALA MARÇAL
CALA FERRERA
SA RAPITA
CALA D'OR
SANTANYÍ
PORTOPETRO
SES SALINES
CALA FIGUERA
CÒLONIA DE SANT JORDI
MEDITERRANEAN SEA
Cap de Ses Salines

Getting to know Mallorca

Mallorca is Europe's favourite holiday destination – and it is easy to see why. A warm climate guarantees sunshine throughout the summer, when the temperatures rise well over 30°C (80°–90°F). Its beaches of pale gold sand are perfect for swimming and sunbathing, while the calm, clear waters and sheltered bays make excellent conditions for water sports. You can eat well with choices ranging from plain grilled fish, straight off the fishing boat, to the finest international cuisine, and the nightlife is some of the hottest in Europe – though if it is peace and quiet you are after, that shouldn't be too hard to find either.

ISLAND OF CONTRASTS

Each of the regions of Mallorca has its own distinct character. The south coast, around the capital, Palma de Mallorca, is where you will find the liveliest resorts as well as some of the island's best beaches – many of which have been awarded the European Union's Blue Flag for their cleanliness and facilities. The north and west coastlines, by contrast, form a region of wild and rugged beauty, dominated by the Serra de Tramuntana mountain range which runs the length of the coast. The north east, around Alcúdia, has some of Mallorca's oldest historical monuments as well as two of the island's longest beaches – while further south, the east coast is studded with tiny *cales*, or pine-fringed coves. At the centre of it all is Es Pla, a fertile plain of almond and apricot groves dotted with solid market towns where life goes on as it always has, as if tourism had never been discovered. And don't forget Palma itself, which is one of the most stylish and cosmopolitan cities in Europe.

SOMETHING FOR EVERYONE

Mallorca has something for everybody – whatever you want from your holiday, you will probably find it here. Children will love the beaches, the water parks and the magic of the sea, and adults can relax knowing that the kids are having fun, while those who like nothing better than lying on a beach, soaking up the sun, will definitely be spoilt for choice.

The best of Mallorca

Here is a checklist of the places you really ought not to miss:

PALMA DE MALLORCA

- **Banys Arabs (Arab Baths)** Dating from the 9th century, these elegant baths survive from Mallorca's long period of Moorish occupation (see page 12).
- **Castell de Bellver (Bellver Castle)** This 14th-century castle on top of a steep hill in Palma now houses the Palma History Museum and is surrounded by a park (see page 14).
- **Cathedral, Almudaina Palace and surrounding areas** The magnificent Gothic cathedral dominates the old quarter of Palma. The interior is richly decorated with works of religious art, illuminated by a stained-glass rose window (see page 14). The Almudaina Palace, next to it, originally the residence of the Moorish kings of Mallorca, is now the official Palma residence of the Spanish king and queen.
- **Coves de Gènova (Caves of Genova)** A fascinating underground cavern complex (see page 16).
- **Mountain train and tram** Take the old wooden train from Palma over the Serra de Tramuntana mountains to Sóller (see page 86). Spectacular views are guaranteed. Then board a historic tram for the final leg of the journey to Port de Sóller (see page 82).

SERRA DE TRAMUNTANA MOUNTAINS

- **Deià** An 'artists' village', where the English writer Robert Graves lived until his death in 1985. He is buried at the hilltop church of Sant Joan Bautista (see page 79).
- **Monastery of Lluc** This venerable monastery is Mallorca's main religious site and an important place of local pilgrimage (see page 87).
- **Torrent de Pareis** The spectacular valley, carved by an ancient river, at Sa Calobra on the coast north of Puerto Sóller, has been described as Mallorca's Grand Canyon (see page 83).
- **Valldemossa** Another attractive old village – Chopin, the Polish

composer, spent a winter at the Charterhouse monastery here in 1838–39 and composed several works (see page 74).

ALCÚDIA & PORT D'ALCÚDIA

- **S'Albufera Natural Park** A wetlands area and wildlife reserve, and an important breeding and staging post for more than 200 species of birds (see page 48).
- **Artà** A beautiful inland town with a remarkable medieval atmosphere. The hilltop Sanctuary of Sant Salvador lies within the walls of the old Moorish citadel (see page 50).
- **Coves d'Artà (Caves of Artà)** Interesting underground formations that lie some 16 km (10 miles) south of the nearby resort of Cala Rajada (see page 50).
- **Historic Alcúdia** Medieval Alcúdia is an atmospheric old town encircled by its defensive walls (see page 44).

CALA D'OR

- **Cala Figuera** One of the prettiest fishing villages in Mallorca. The fishermen's houses line the banks of the narrow cala, or bay, on which the village stands, and each one has a boathouse built beside it (see page 67).

PORTO CRISTO

- **Coves del Drach (Dragon Caves)** The most spectacular underground caverns in Mallorca, containing one of the biggest underground lakes in the world (see page 58). The nearby Coves dels Hams (Caves of Hams) are not as big but are still impressive (see page 58).
- **Mallorca Aquarium** Display tanks depict scenes from Pacific coral reefs, Brazilian rivers, and the Mediterranean sea (see page 58).

RESORTS
Places under the sun

Palma de Mallorca (Palma Town)
cosmopolitan capital

Palma de Mallorca, beautifully situated at the centre of Palma Bay, is the capital of the Balearic Islands. This vibrant, cosmopolitan city has managed to retain a great deal of its ancient charm. Its bustling street life and thriving arts scene lead many people to compare it with the stylish Catalan capital, Barcelona, and it was recently chosen by a leading Spanish newspaper as the best place to live in Spain.

The most striking image of Palma is its cathedral, standing proud on the waterfront and seeming almost to grow out of the sea. Behind the cathedral is the old Arab quarter, a warren of narrow lanes shielding ancient palaces and mansions, with elegant courtyards featuring stone stairways and potted plants. A short stroll from here leads to **Plaça Major**, a pleasant square of open-air cafés, at the heart of the pedestrian shopping district with its many small speciality shops. Amble down **La Rambla**, with its dozens of flower-sellers, and the tree-lined **Passeig des Born**, to return to the waterfront where the real life-blood of Palma lies. Fishermen mend their nets, cruise ships drift into the harbour, and the designer bars along the **Passeig Marítim** buzz with conversation after dark.

Take a ride around the old town in a *galera* (horse and carriage). A list of prices is displayed at the various carriage ranks around town, but if you are happy with the service the drivers never refuse a tip.

THINGS TO SEE & DO

Banys Arabs (Arab Baths) ★★

The ornate columns and elegant domes of these baths, dating from the 10th century, are one of the few surviving monuments from Mallorca's long period of Moorish rule. Carrer Serra 7 971 72 15 49 Open 09.30–18.30 Admission charge

PALMA DE MALLORCA
AVINGUDA GABRIEL ALOMAR I VILLALONGA
MATEU ENRIC LLADO
PARC DE LA MAR
PLAÇA SANT FRANCESC
PLAÇA MAJOR
PLAÇA SANTA EULALIA
JAUME II
SANT BARTOMEU
MOREY
PALAU
CARRER OMS
LA RAMBLA
CARRER UNIO
CARRER CONQUISTADOR
MIRADOR
SANT JAUME
PASSEIG DES BORN
AV. ANTONI MAURA
AUTOPISTA DE LEVANTE
AVINGUDA JAUME III
PASSEIG MALLORCA
PASSEIG MALLORCA
AVINGUDA DE 'L ARGENTINA
AVINGUDA GABRIEL ROCA (PASSEIG MARITIM)
CONTRAMOLL MOLLET
RER INDUSTRIA
ESPARTERO COMTE DE BARCELONA
SANT MAGI
PLAÇA PONT
JOAN CRESPI
MARQUES DE LA SENIA
BARTOMEU
SON COTONERET
CARRER ANDREA DORIA
ROSSELLO-PORCEL
FEDERICO GARCIA LORCA
AVINGUDA JOAN MIRO
PLAÇA ALM CHURRUCA
AVINGUDA GABRIEL ROCA
PLAÇA GOMILA
AV. JOAN MIRO
CARRER ANDREA DORIA
PARC DE BELLVER
CASTELL DE BELLVER
DOS DE MAIG
MEDITERRANEAN SEA
1 LA LLOTJA
2 FUNDACIÓ LA CAIXA
3 BANYS ARABS
4 THEATRE
5 FUNDACIÓ JUAN MARCH
6 PLAÇA D'ESPANYA
N
0 250 500 m
0 0.25 mile

Castell de Bellver (Bellver Castle) ★★

This circular castle, high in the woods above Palma Bay, was built in the 14th century soon after the Catalan conquest. It also houses the Palma History Museum. ⓐ Parc Bellver (take a taxi from Palma or bus no. 3 and walk) ⓣ 971 73 06 57 ⓒ Open Mon–Sat 08.00–20.00, Sun 10.00-17.00 (Oct–Mar); Mon–Sat 08.00– 21.00, Sun 10.00-19.00 (Apr–Jun, Sept); Mon–Sat 08.00–21.00, Sun 10.00-14.00 and 16.00–20.00 (July-Aug) ⓘ Admission charge

---

Visit one of Palma's four city tourist offices – in the Plaça d'Espanya, Plaça de la Reina 2, Passeig des Born 27 and Carrer Sant Domingo, in the old town – for up-to-date information on local events.

Cathedral ★★★

Palma's marvellous Gothic cathedral occupies a prominent position overlooking the sea at the edge of the old city. It was begun in the 13th century but has been extensively remodelled over the years, most recently by the famous Catalan architect Antoni Gaudí at the start of

SHOPPING

Serious shoppers should head for **Avinguda Jaume III**, where most of the city's boutiques are situated. Here you can find leather goods, designer clothes, jewellery and antiques as well as a branch of Spain's top department store, **El Corte Inglés**. Those who enjoy browsing in small, specialist shops should make for the area around **Plaça Major**.

Markets: Palma's main market is held six mornings a week (not Sundays) in the Olivar market hall near **Plaça d'Espanya**. A *baratillo* (flea market) takes place each Saturday morning on the ring road at **Avinguda Gabriel Alomar i Villalonga**. There is also a lively open-air craft market during the week in the Plaça Major.

the 20th century. Plaça Almoina s/n Open Mon–Fri 10.00–18.15, Sat 10.00–14.15 (summer), 10.00–14.30 (winter), closed Sun (except for High Mass at 10.30, 12.00, 13.00 and 19.00) Admission charge

Fundació La Caixa (La Caixa Gallery) ★★

This art gallery in the former Gran Hotel has a permanent exhibition of Mallorcan paintings as well as changing temporary displays. The ground-floor café is one of Palma's smartest meeting-spots, and the building itself, a fine example of Catalan Modernist architecture, is also worth a look. Plaça Weyler 3 971 72 01 11 Open Tues–Sat 10.00–21.00, Sun 10.00–14.00 Free admission

Fundació Juan March (Juan March Gallery) ★★

This small but dazzling display of contemporary Spanish art includes some treasures by Picasso, Salvador Dalí and Miró. Carrer de Sant Miquel 11 971 71 35 15 www.march.es/arte/ingles/palma Open Mon–Fri 10.00–18.30, Sat 10.00–14.00 Free admission

Passeig Marítim (seafront promenade) ★★

Starting near the cathedral, stroll the length of the Passeig Marítim past the small traditional fishing port (the Port de Pesca) and the seemingly endless rows of luxury yachts and motorboats to the Estació Marítimo (the ship terminal) at the far end, where naval ships, cruise liners and ferries from mainland Spain dock – and you will soon appreciate Palma's long-standing love affair with the sea. Plenty of bars and restaurants for refreshments as you go.

The *Majorca Daily Bulletin*, a newspaper published in English six times a week, is a Palma institution. You can buy it at news-stands all over the city, or pick up a copy at one of the tourist offices.

La Rambla ★

La Rambla has been one of the city's main promenades for years. This tree-lined avenue is filled with the stalls of Palma's daily flower market.

Palma's cathedral

EXCURSIONS

Coves de Gènova (Caves of Genova) ★★

These spectacular caves can be found in the charming village of Gènova, high on the slopes of the Serra de Na Burguesa hills above Palma, and easily reached on bus no. 4. Ⓐ Carrer de Barranc 45 Ⓣ 971 40 23 87 Ⓛ Open 10.00–13.30 and 16.00–19.00 (summer), 10.30–13.00 and 16.00–18.00 (winter) ⓘ Admission charge

Festival Park ★

This spacious leisure complex has an enormous range of facilities and activities on offer. There are 29 different shops and factory outlets, 30 restaurants, including Chinese, Greek and Italian, two cinemas, 22-lane bowling, not to mention the largest reptilarium in Europe. Enjoy evening open-air entertainment in the centre square or visit the summer crafts market. Ⓐ Palma–Inca road just before Santa Maria, take the train from Plaça Espanya, Palma to Marratxi, then a 5-minute walk Ⓦ www.festivalparks.com Ⓛ Shops open 10.00–2200; park open until early hours; summer market open Fri–Sat 18.00–23.00

Fundació Pilar i Joan Miró (Pilar and Juan Miró Gallery) ★★★
The abstract Catalan artist Joan Miró lived on Mallorca for much of his life and his house and studio have been turned into a museum of his work. The studio itself has been left largely untouched since his death in 1983, with tins of paint still lying around open on the tables. Carrer Joan de Saridakis 29, Cala Major (taxi or buses no. 3, 4 and 21 from Palma) 971 70 14 20 Open Tues–Sat 10.00–19.00 (summer), 10.00–18.00 (winter), Sun 10.00–15.00; closed Mon Admission charge

Ocimax ★
The leisure centre in Palma has 15 cinema screens and 26-lane bowling. Wide choice of restaurants and bars. Gymnasium and children's play park. Ample parking. Opposite Carrefour Hypermarket

Puerto Portals ★★★
The St Tropez of the Balearics and Mallorca's most glamorous resort. Its glitzy marina, crammed with fashionable restaurants and bars, is a great venue for people-watching and celebrity-spotting.

RESTAURANTS & BARS (see map on page 13)

Abaco €€ ❶ Palma's most unusual cocktail bar is situated inside a 17th-century palace, with caged birds, fountains, classical music and huge baskets of fruit. Carrer Sant Joan 1 971 71 49 39 Open 20.00–01.30, Fri and Sat 20.00–03.30

Arrocería Ca Cranca €€ ❷ The speciality at this restaurant on the seafront is paella, freshly cooked to order and served in a number of different styles, including vegetarian. Passeig Marítim 13 971 73 74 47 Open Tues–Sat 13.00–15.30 and 20.00–23.30

Baisakhi €€ ❸ This high-class Indian restaurant on the waterfront has developed an excellent reputation over the years. New menu chosen by the owner every day. Passeig Marítim 8 971 73 68 06 Open Tues–Sun, two sittings: 20.00 and 23.00

Bar Bosch € ❹ This café-bar at the top of the Passeig des Born has long been one of the city's most popular meeting places. ⓐ Plaça Rei Joan Carles I ⓣ 971 72 11 31 ⓛ Open 08.00–03.00; closed Sun

Bon Lloc € ❺ This vegetarian restaurant is popular for its good-value four-course set menu. ⓐ Carrer Sant Feliu 7 ⓣ 971 71 86 17 ⓛ Open Tues–Sat 13.00–16.00 and Fri 21.00–midnight

La Bóveda €€ ❻ This is definitely the best and most popular tapas bar in Palma. Choose from *pa amb oli* (open sandwiches topped with ham or cheese), cured ham, mussels and octopus, which you eat while standing up against an old wine barrel. ⓐ Carrer Botería 3 ⓣ 971 71 48 63 ⓛ Open Mon–Sat 13.30–16.00 and 20.30–00.30

Caballito de Mar €€€ ❼ Fresh fish and seafood dishes, such as sea bass baked in rock salt, are the specialities at this busy seafront restaurant. ⓐ Passeig Sagrera 5 ⓣ 971 72 10 74 ⓛ Open 13.00–16.00 and 20.00–midnight; closed Mon

Ca'n Joan de S'Aigo € ❽ Pastries, cakes, almond ice cream and scrumptious hot chocolate are on the menu at this 200-year- old café in a narrow winding street. ⓐ Carrer Ca'n Sanc 10 ⓣ 971 72 57 60 ⓛ Open 08.00–21.00 and Sat and Sun 08.00–21.30; closed Tues

Es Parlement €€ ❾ Located in the Balearic Parliament buildings, this traditional restaurant reputedly serves the best *paella ciega* ('blind paella' – without the bones) in town. ⓐ Carrer de Conquistador 11 ⓣ 971 72 60 26 ⓛ Open Mon–Sat 13.00-16.00 and 20.00-23.00

El Patio € ❿ This delightful courtyard restaurant serves a variety of fresh pasta dishes, as well as salads and grilled meat and fish. ⓐ Carrer dels Apuntadors 3 ⓣ 971 71 17 68 ⓛ Open Mon–Sat 13.00–15.30 and 19.30–midnight

Port Pesquer €€ ⓫ The latest addition to Palma's waterfront is this chic café with live music on Thurs and Fri, great tapas served from midday to midnight, and wonderful harbour views. ⓐ Passeig Marítim, near the fishing port ⓣ 971 71 52 20 ⓛ Open 09.00–03.00

Sa Premsa €€ ⓬ This is a typical Mallorcan cellar-restaurant, in a converted garage with wine vats around the walls. The food is cheap and rustic, with the emphasis on dishes such as *frito mallorquín* (see page 94) and pork wrapped in cabbage leaves. Cheerful service; old bullfight posters on walls. ⓐ Plaça Bisbe Berenguer de Palou 8 ⓣ 971 72 35 29 ⓛ Open Mon–Sat 12.30–16.00 and 19.30–23.30

Shogun €€ ⓭ One of Mallorca's most popular Japanese restaurants, a graceful place below the Bellver Castle. ⓐ Carrer Camilo José Cela 14 ⓣ 971 73 57 48 ⓛ Open 13.00–15.30 and 20.00–23.30

La Taberna del Caracol €€ ⓮ In one of the oldest buildings in the Old Quarter, serving outstanding tapas with an enormous variety. Sample one or two or try the house speciality which includes a little of everything. ⓐ San Alonso 2, Plaça de Mallorca ⓣ 971 71 49 08 ⓛ Open Mon–Sat 13.00–15.30 and 19.00–23.00

NIGHTLIFE

Most of the late-night action in Palma takes place along the Passeig Marítim. Teenagers head for **Pacha**, the latest disco hotspot (ⓛ Open 23.00–06.00) while a slightly older crowd gathers at **Tito's**, Palma's largest nightclub, with six bars, a laser show and great views over the bay (ⓛ Open 22.00–06.00, ⓐ Use the outdoor lifts from Passeig Marítim).

Son Amar Mallorca's top nightspot lies just outside Palma, in a converted 16th-century mansion on the road to Sóller. The cabaret show here features flamenco and Spanish ballet, as well as magicians, flying dancers and a live concert by a cover band. It's definitely a night to remember. Ask your holiday representative for details of excursions. ⓐ Carretera de Sóller, Km 10, Bunyola ⓣ 971 61 75 33

Illetes
relaxing beach resort

Illetes takes its name from the pair of rocky islets that can be seen just offshore. This quiet, low-key resort, with two good beaches overlooking Palma Bay, is a Spanish residential area and also a popular weekend outing for families from Palma – with the result that it is by far the most Spanish of the Bay of Palma resorts.

Trying to find a convenient parking space in Illetes can be a nightmare. There is a large new free car park but it is not close to the beach and has numerous steps. It is much easier to arrive on the regular buses from Palma, with connections to all the other south coast resorts.

BEACHES

The main beach, **Platja d'Illetes**, is right in the centre of the resort and has plenty of sunbeds and parasols for hire as well as several snack bars right beside the sea. A short walk leads past the tiny **Platja Cala Comptessa** to **Platja d'Illetes III**, which is quieter with fewer facilities.

RESTAURANTS & BARS

Stroll along to San Augustin with a wealth of choice. Easy parking too, if you decide to take the car! Excellent French, Chinese and and Indian restaurants, and there's even a Russian one if you fancy something a little different.

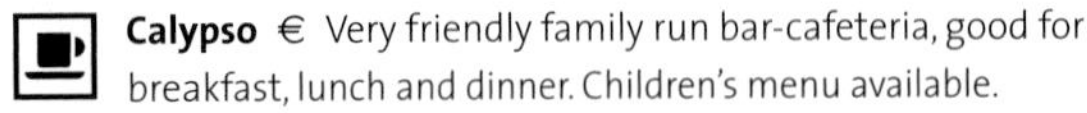

Calypso € Very friendly family run bar-cafeteria, good for breakfast, lunch and dinner. Children's menu available.
Ⓐ Paseig d'Illetes 22 Ⓞ Open Tues–Sun 10.00–late

Illetes Playa €€ An excellent Mallorcan restaurant with an international flavour and a generally upmarket, formal approach. The house speciality is a mixed seafood grill. Ⓐ Passeig d'Illetes 75 Ⓣ 971 70 18 96 Ⓞ Open 13.00–16.30 and 19.00–23.00

Es Parral €€ Chicken Mallorcan style is the speciality at this popular restaurant above the beach. Passeig d'Illetes 75 971 70 11 27 Open 12.30–16.00 and 18.00–midnight

The Rose Mallow € This olde-worlde English pub has lots of character, friendly staff, and afternoon cream teas with home-made cakes and scones. Passeig d'Illetes 4 971 40 18 81 Open 11.00–23.00

La Solara €€ The perfect place for a lazy lunch on the beach – paella, snacks and sandwiches served on a shady terrace beside the sea. Platja d'Illetes 971 40 27 47 Open 10.00–19.00

NIGHTLIFE

Virtual Club Think of this as a sophisticated Flintstones experience! A spectacular bar, set in natural caves beside the sea, attached to a restaurant and beach club with music until the early hours. Passeig d'Illetes 60 971 70 32 35 www.virtualclub.es Open 12.00–02.00

Beach at Illetes

Palma Nova
family fun

Palma Nova (New Palma), beautifully situated on a wide, sandy bay, was one of Mallorca's earliest tourist resorts. Sandwiched between the ritzy harbour at Puerto Portals and the riotous nightlife of Magaluf, Palma Nova remains an excellent resort for families, with golden beaches, a wide choice of restaurants and two of Mallorca's leading family attractions.

THINGS TO SEE & DO

Golf ★

Of all the mini-golf courses in Mallorca, **Golf Fantasia**, set amid waterfalls, caves and tropical gardens, is one of the best. There is a choice of three different courses – or you can stay all day and play all 54 holes.
ⓐ Carrer Tenis 3 ⓣ 971 13 50 40 ◷ Open 10.00–02.00
ⓦ www.golf-fantasia.com ❶ Admission charge

Sea-life centre ★★

Performing dolphins, sea lions and parrots are the star turns at the **Marineland** centre, just along the coast from Palma Nova at Portals Nous. There is also a penguin pool, a reptile house and an aquarium with sharks and tropical fish on display. Children can have fun in the adventure playground or take a ride on a mock pirate boat – a great day out for all the family. Ask your holiday representative for details of excursions.
ⓐ Carretera Palma–Andratx ⓣ 971 67 51 25 ⓦ www.marineland.es
◷ Dolphin shows 11.30, 15.00 and 17.30. Parrot shows 10.30, 13.00, 16.45
❶ Admission charge (free for under-3s, special price 3–12 year-olds)

BEACHES

The main beach at Palma Nova is divided into two sections, both well equipped with sunbeds, showers, lifeguards and warning flags. A third beach, Son Maties, lies just around the bay – from here it is a short walk to the beach at Magaluf (page 24).

RESTAURANTS

La Cucaracha €€ Palma Nova's only Mexican restaurant, serving fajitas, nachos and other Mexican specialities, is worth a visit for its excellent cooking and high standard of service. Ⓐ Passeig de la Mar 20 Ⓣ 971 68 30 45 Ⓛ Open Sun–Thurs 18.00–midnight, Fri and Sat 12.30–midnight

Marbella Club € British steak house serving traditional fare including English breakfasts, Sunday lunches and vegetarian dishes. The atmosphere is relaxed, lively and fun and there is a bar and games room. Ⓐ Carrer Miguel de los Santos Oliver 10 Ⓣ 971 68 31 54 Ⓛ Open 11.00–12.30 and 15.00–late (20.00 Sun); closed Mon lunch

Real Dion €€ A top-quality British-run restaurant serving imaginative home-cooked food. The house speciality is roast lamb, but the more adventurous can try salmon in champagne sauce followed by raspberry brûlée. Ⓐ Passeig de la Mar 16 Ⓣ 971 68 24 57 Ⓛ Open 19.00–midnight (summer); Thur–Sun evenings only (winter)

NIGHTLIFE

Pub Papis Bar with food served during the day. Wide variety of music and themed nights which are very popular with the young crowd, although things don't really start to warm up until after 22.00 and then the atmosphere becomes electric!
Ⓐ Carrer Pedro Vaquer 2
Ⓣ 971 68 30 96
Ⓛ Open 06.00–04.00
Ⓘ Admission free

Beach at Palma Nova

Magaluf
Mallorca's nightlife capital

Magaluf, more than anywhere else, exemplifies the rapid growth of Mallorcan tourism. What was once no more than a quiet fishing village surrounded by marshes on the edge of Palma Bay has been transformed over the last 40 years into a pulsating mega-resort.

The beach, with its stylish seafront promenade, is one of the best on the island and, if you fancy something more energetic than sunbathing, there are canoes and pedal boats for hire – as well as windsurfing and snorkelling equipment. But most visitors to Magaluf save their energy for the legendary round-the-clock nightlife. From discos and cocktail bars to rip-roaring dinner shows and dubious 'adult entertainment', Magaluf has it all. And you do not even have to go far to escape the crowds. A bumpy track through pine woods from the edge of the resort leads to the peaceful resort of Cala Vinyes with its sandy coves and stunning views.

THINGS TO SEE & DO

Aqualand Magaluf ★★

A giant water park with death-defying slides, thrilling rides for older kids and some tamer ones for the toddlers. ⓐ Carretera de Cala Figuera, on the edge of Magaluf ⓣ 971 13 08 11 ⓦ www.aqualand.es/magaluf/mallorca ⓛ Open 10.00–18.00 (17.00 winter) ⓘ Admission charge

Bungee Rocket ★

Try this if you fancy being the ammunition in a human slingshot! ⓐ Carrer Punta Ballena, Magaluf ⓛ Open summer months only

Go-karting ★

Older children in particular will enjoy racing around the **Karting Magaluf** track on the outskirts of the resort. ⓐ Camino de sa Porrassa (next to Aquapark) ⓣ 971 13 17 34 ⓦ www.kartingmagaluf.com ⓛ Open 10.00–midnight (July/August); rest of year 10.00–sunset

Submarine trip ★★

A 50-minute underwater excursion in a genuine submarine is the highlight of the **Nemo Submarine** two-hour trip from Magaluf. Panoramic portholes allow you to view the underwater wildlife and shipwrecks (Ⓐ Carrer Galió 2 Ⓣ 971 13 02 44 Ⓛ Open 09.00–20.00 Ⓘ Children under 3 not allowed). **Neptuno-Sub** is a cruise around the south-west coast on a triple-deck catamaran with underwater viewing windows. Trips leave three times a day from Magaluf beach (Ⓣ 971 13 12 11 for reservations).

BEACHES

Magaluf's beach runs parallel to the main street of the resort and is never more than a short walk away. Also within walking distance is **Platja Son Maties**, on the edge of the neighbouring resort of Palma Nova (see map page 26). Portals Vells, on the headland south of Magaluf, has two small beaches including **Platja Mago**, one of Mallorca's official nudist beaches.

RESTAURANTS & BARS (see map on page 26)

Los Caracoles €€ ❶ A traditional Spanish restaurant known for its excellent steaks. Ⓐ Galerías Joboso, Carrer Martín Ros García Ⓣ 971 68 02 67 Ⓛ Open Tues–Sun 12.30–midnight

Cottage € ❷ Family orientated with brilliant breakfasts and meals and snacks throughout the day. Music, films and football matches. Ⓐ Avinguda S'Olivera 9 Ⓣ 971 13 20 37 Ⓛ Open 09.00–late (kitchen closes 23.00)

Eastenders € ❸ 'Just like home' is the promise of this very English restaurant, where roast beef and Yorkshire pudding take top billing. Ⓐ Carrer Pinada 6 Ⓣ 971 68 26 17 Ⓛ Open 09.00–03.30

Mrs Doyle's € ❹ Irish pub food all day and buzzing in the evening with a fiddler and other entertainment, followed by a disco. Very friendly. Ⓐ Carrer Galió 51 Ⓛ Open 10.00–02.00 Mar–Oct

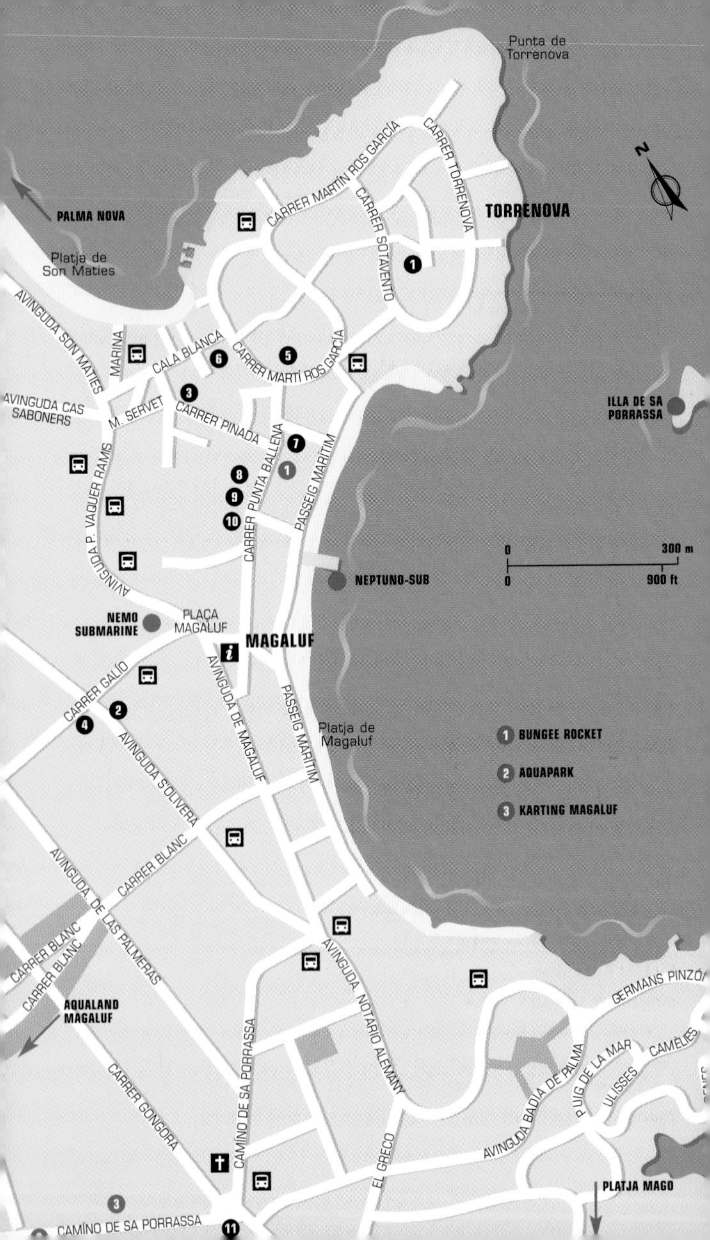
Punta de Torrenova
TORRENOVA
PALMA NOVA
Platja de Son Maties
Carrer Martín Ros García
Carrer Torrenova
Carrer Sotavento
Avinguda Son Maties
Marina
Cala Blanca
Carrer Martí Ros García
Avinguda Cas Saboners
M. Servet
Carrer Pinada
Carrer Punta Ballena
Passeig Marítim
Avinguda P. Vaquer Ramis
ILLA DE SA PORRASSA
NEPTUNO-SUB
0 300 m
0 900 ft
NEMO SUBMARINE
Plaça Magaluf
MAGALUF
Carrer Galío
Avinguda de Magaluf
Passeig Marítim
Platja de Magaluf
Avinguda S'Olivera
1 BUNGEE ROCKET
2 AQUAPARK
3 KARTING MAGALUF
Carrer Blanc
Avinguda de las Palmeras
Carrer Blanc
Carrer Blanc
AQUALAND MAGALUF
Avinguda Notario Alemany
Germans Pinzó
Camino de Sa Porrassa
Carrer Gongora
Avinguda Badia de Palma
Puig de la Mar
Ulisses
Camelies
El Greco
PLATJA MAGO
Camíno de Sa Porrassa

Pachas Pub € ❺ One of the best-known cocktail bars in Magaluf, famed for its cocktails, served in quantities of up to five litres. Electrifying atmosphere. ⓐ Carrer Martí Ros García 12 Ⓛ Open 12.00–04.00

El Salmon €€ ❻ This was the first restaurant in Magaluf and it is still known for its well-presented Mallorcan and international cuisine. The atmosphere is elegant but relaxed. ⓐ Carrer Cala Blanca 10 ⓣ 971 68 00 10 Ⓛ Open 12.00–14.00 and 18.00–01.00, Sun 18.00–01.00

NIGHTLIFE (see map on page 26)

Channis or **Bar 29** (opposite BCM) are popular pre-club bars to start off the night. **BCM** is outrageously huge! Top international DJs come here to do their thing. The most spectacular lighting systems in Europe are on the upper level. The middle level attracts a marginally older set and the **Millennium** in the basement is worth a look for its nightly foam parties. They also have popcorn parties. Smart but casual dress. Age range 16–30. ⓐ All four can be found on Avinguda S'Olivera 2

Boomerang ❼ A modern disco with wide range of dance and party music and very lively atmosphere, which has three bars. ⓐ Carrer Miguel Altoaguirre 1 ⓦ www.boomerangnightclub.com Ⓛ Open 22.00–07.00

Tokio Joe's ❽ House and garage music with six large bars.
Fusion ❾ All-night disco with pop and chart sounds.
The Venue ❿ Great open-plan club with funky music and friendly service. ⓐ All three clubs can be found on Carrer Punta Ballena

Pirates Adventure ⓫ A great family night out, with a swashbuckling pirates adventure show. Audience participation is encouraged, with free-flowing Pirate Punch to loosen your inhibitions. Booking strongly advised – see your holiday rep for details. ⓐ Carretera de sa Porrassa ⓣ 971 13 04 11 ⓦ www.piratesadventure.com Ⓛ Family show 18.00 and 20.00, family matinée 15.00. Adult show 21.00 and 23.00 (times may vary)

Torrenova
round-the-clock fun

The Torrenova area is a fun-orientated district of Magaluf with lots of things to see and do right around the clock – suitable for young people and families alike. Torrenova enjoys a prime position, acting as the centre for both Palma Nova and Magaluf. Dance the night away in the district's many discos and bars, or just relax and chill out in its quieter outskirts.

THINGS TO SEE & DO

Boat trips ★★

Numerous boat excursions can be taken around the local bays, providing glimpses of the local marine life that Mallorca has to offer.

Cycling ★

Hire a bike for an hour or a day. Pepe has tandems, tricycles and even family-sized 'safari' bikes. ⓐ Carrer Cala Blanca ⓣ 971 68 03 14 ⓒ Open 08.00–22.00

Water sports ★

Torrenova offers an extensive selection of water sports, based on Son Maties beach. You can experience the breeze in your hair while on skis, or relax underwater while diving to the shallow depths of the warm and calm waters. **Big Blue Divers** ⓐ Carrer Martí Ros García 6 ⓣ 971 68 16 86

RESTAURANTS & BARS

Dauphine € Friendly beach restaurant, serving tortilla, sardines and other light meals. ⓐ Playa de Magaluf ⓣ 971 68 07 86 ⓒ Open 09.00–02.00

Nawaab Indian Restaurant €€ Find all your favourite Indian dishes as mild or hot as you like. Take-aways too. ⓐ Calle Pineda (next to Bungee Rocket) ⓣ 971 13 09 34 ⓒ Open 17.00–01.00

The Prince William € A large pub, popular with British visitors to the resort. Calle Pinada 1 Open 365 days a year 11.00–05.00

Robin Hood € Friendly local restaurant serving home-cooked British food. Extensive menu served with a friendly smile. Great breakfasts! Carrer Sant Miquel de Liria 10 971 68 34 37 Open 09.00–23.00 (May–Oct)

Ruby Tuesdays €€ Diner, including kids' meals, with karaoke and other pub fun. Chill out on the terrace bar with the spectacular views over Palma Nova and Palma Bay. Carrer Martí Ros García 971 68 33 63 Open 10.00–02.00

NIGHTLIFE

The resort is a 24-hour happening place. Lively bars and discos include:

Banana Techno/house/garage music. Mermaids swim in a glass pool. Carrer Martí Ros García 2 Open 22.30–06.00 Admission charge

Carwash The dancing staff wear 1970s clothes but the music ranges from 1970s and 1980s to the latest sounds. Dress style is casual. Garci de Ruiz 11 971 68 34 07 Open 22.00–06.00 Admission charge

Poco Loco Great party atmosphere, resident British DJ and commercial dance music. Carrer Martí Ros García 5 Open 10.00–06.00

SHOPPING

Marina Shopping Centre Offering restaurants, boutiques, perfume, jewellery and sports shops, all at tax-free prices.

Punta Balena main strip Local products, souvenir shops, jewellers, shoe shops, boutiques, supermarkets, perfumeries – anything you want is along this main strip.

Santa Ponça
historic spot

Santa Ponça is a lively resort on the south-west coast, built around a marina and an excellent beach. Despite its modern appearance, the town has an important place in Mallorcan history, commemorated by the large cross above the marina, which marks the spot where Jaume I landed in 1229 at the beginning of his successful campaign to drive the Moors from the island. It was this invasion that paved the way for Mallorca to become a part of modern Spain.

When the sun gets too hot you can retreat to the shade of the wooded park behind the beach (picnicking is not allowed here).

THINGS TO SEE & DO

Scuba diving ★

If you want to try your hand at scuba diving, **Centro de Buceo Zoea** offers equipment hire and tuition. ⓐ Club Náutico Santa Ponça ⓣ 971 69 14 44 ⓦ www.zoea.com

Golf ★

The most challenging golf course on Mallorca, **Golf Santa Ponça** has been home to the Balearic Open. The course features long, wide fairways set amid pretty countryside dotted with almond and olive trees. Club and trolley hire available. ⓐ Urbanización Santa Ponça, Palma-Andratx Road, Km 18, just outside the resort ⓣ 971 69 02 11 ⓑ Open all year

BEACHES

The main beach, a horseshoe of golden sand, lies close to the centre of the resort and offers a variety of water sports. A smaller beach, set in its own sheltered cove, can be reached from Avinguda Rei Jaume I, about a 15-minute walk from the main beach. From here it is a short stroll to the Creu de la Conquesta (Conquest Cross), with panoramic views over the bay.

RESTAURANTS & BARS

Jaggy Thistle € This Scottish pub caters for football fans with entertainment nightly from 22.00, followed by the legendary 'Jaggy Karaoki'. Ⓐ Avinguda Rei Jaume I Ⓣ 971 69 57 70 Ⓛ Open 19.00–02.00

Mesón del Rey €€ A typically Spanish restaurant in a quiet back street away from the tourist zone. There are pavement tables and the atmosphere is relaxed and friendly. Prices are reasonable and the paella is particularly good. Ⓐ Carrer Puig des Teix Ⓣ 971 69 08 15 Ⓛ Open 13.00–16.00 and 19.00–midnight

Beach terrace at Santa Ponça

Restaurante Oeste €€ The ultimate dining experience with such delicacies as kangaroo, ostrich and wild boar. But such traditional dishes as sirloin steak are second to none, as are the pizzas and pastas. Ⓐ Avinguda Rei Jaume 1, 84 Santa Ponça Ⓣ 971 69 02 66 Ⓛ Open 12.30–15.30 and 19.00–midnight (summer); closed winter

Simsalabim € Sample pizzas with such evocative names as Desert Storm or Eastern Promise in an incredible setting decorated to resemble a nomad's tent from the Arabian Nights. Ⓐ Avinguda Jaume I, Santa Ponça Ⓣ 971 69 78 04 Ⓛ Open 12.00–midnight

NIGHTLIFE

Fama This nightclub is particularly popular at weekends with older clubbers as well as the younger crowd. Spanish/international disco. No dress code. Ⓐ Carrer Ramón de Montcada 2 Ⓣ 971 69 33 16 Ⓛ Open midnight–06.00 Ⓘ Admission free

Peguera
beach retreat

Peguera is a small but bustling beach resort set around a clear turquoise bay with a pair of golden sandy beaches. This area has become particularly popular with German visitors in recent years. The coast road from Peguera to Camp de Mar continues over the mountains to the glitzy marina at Port d'Andratx, another popular hangout for Mallorca's visiting jet set (page 34).

THINGS TO SEE & DO

Glass-bottomed boats ★★

Trips leave regularly from Peguera for Camp de Mar and Port d'Andratx. Some of the trips continue to the village of Sant Elm and the offshore island of Sa Dragonera, now a nature reserve.

BEACHES

Peguera's main beach forms a wide arc of fine sand, with restaurants lining the seafront promenade and plenty of sunbeds and sunshades available for hire. An easy walk of about half an hour leads to the tiny beach at Cala Fornells, beautifully situated inside a crystal-clear cove.

RESTAURANTS & BARS

Ambassador €€ This upmarket restaurant specialises in seafood, with grilled monkfish and prawns flambéed in whisky among the house specialities. Only wood-burning oven in Peguera: shoulder of lamb, suckling pig, baby goat. Ⓐ Avinguda de Peguera 68 Ⓣ 971 68 60 06 Ⓛ Open 11.00–16.00 and 18.30–23.30

Amigos Mexican Restaurant €€ Pop in for a jacket potato filled with chili con carne and topped with cheese and guacamole sauce and be out in half an hour, or sit down to a full three-course meal for hours on end and enjoy the atmosphere. Ⓐ Ramon de Moncada 24, Peguera Ⓣ 971 69 35 15 Ⓛ Open 18.30–midnight

Es Fasset € A German beer garden with an outdoor, country feel. The restaurant serves pizzas and pasta dishes and the cellar disco plays a mix of English, Spanish and German music. Carrer Eucaliptus 5 971 68 71 71 Open 10.00–02.00 (live music from 20.00) Admission free

La Gran Tortuga €€ Try monkfish stuffed with smoked salmon in spinach sauce. Lovely terrace snack bar. Cala Fornells 971 68 60 23 13.00–15.30 and 19.30–23.00

La Gritta €€ Smart Italian restaurant with stunning views from its terrace and food to match. Its menu ranges from classic Spanish dishes such as sea bream baked in a salt crust to Italian specialities like *pansoti*, pasta stuffed with spinach and cheese. Carrer L'Espiga 9, Cala Fornells 971 68 60 22 Open 13.00–15.30 and 19.30–23.30

NIGHTLIFE

Paladium Palace 'We heat up when the sun goes down' promises this nightspot that appeals mostly to the younger crowd, though that can stretch from 18 to 35. Spectacular sound system laser show. A varied programme of dance music goes along with foam parties and theme nights. Dress is casual. Carrer Gaviotas 1 971 68 65 57 Open 22.00–06.00 Admission free

SHOPPING

Cambalache This is a long street lined with shops ranging from the trendiest designer fashions to leather accessories, jewellery and arts and crafts.

Le Pirat Jeans are a good buy at this trendy designer-label clothes store on the main street. Ctra. Andratx 3 971 68 53 81

Port d'Andratx
stylish port

Port d'Andratx (pronounced 'an-dratch') was once a humble fishing village but today it is one of Mallorca's most fashionable resorts, and a great favourite with the yachting fraternity. The picturesque hilly countryside surrounding the port, rich with peach trees, olive groves and vineyards, is also well worth exploring.

Port d'Andratx's character stems from its deep natural harbour – one of the most popular moorings in Mallorca – and its quaysides, lined by all types of craft from traditional fishing boats to massive yachts and ostentatious gin palaces. There is nothing more enjoyable than strolling along the waterfront here, shopping in the chic boutiques, or whiling away the day in one of the sophisticated harbourside restaurants and bars, people-watching and maybe even celebrity-spotting.

The resort also offers visitors a huge range of water sports, but don't come here if you are looking for beaches because you will be disappointed! The best beaches nearby are a short distance along the coast in the neighbouring resorts of **Camp de Mar** and **Sant Elm** (see opposite). They are easily reached by boat from Port d'Andratx.

Just 4 km (2½ miles) inland, the hilltop town of **Andratx**, surrounded by almond and orange groves, is a must-see. This sleepy town was built away from the coast as a precaution against pirate attack. During the Middle Ages it was the home of both the Catalan King Jaume I and the Bishop of Barcelona, hence the massive fortress-like church of Santa María high atop the old town, which commands dazzling views.

On Wednesday mornings Andratx comes alive with one of Mallorca's biggest country markets. It is a good place to pick up food for a picnic.

The best time to visit Port d'Andratx is just before sunset when the string of popular waterfront cafés and tapas bars which line the promenade come alive and the light is at its best for photographers.

THINGS TO SEE & DO

Boat trips ★★

Hop on a pleasure cruiser and visit the neighbouring resorts of Camp de Mar and Sant Elm, both with their golden sandy beaches. Or try a voyage further afield and take a day trip to Magaluf and Palma Nova. There are also frequent boat trips to the island of Sa Dragonera.

Walks ★

Ask in the Tourist Office for their leaflet on walks around Andratx and explore the countryside. The coastal walks are particularly enjoyable.

Scuba diving ★

This part of the coastline offers some of the best scuba diving in Mallorca, with daily courses for both advanced divers and beginners at **Aqua Marine Diving**. ⓐ Carrer Almirante Riera Alemany 23 ⓣ 971 67 43 76

EXCURSIONS

Banyalbufar ★★

The road between Andratx and the small farming community of Banyalbufar is one of the best scenic drives in Mallorca, twisting through pretty mountain hamlets high above the craggy northern coastline.

Camp de Mar ★★

This low-key holiday resort with its golf club (see page 104 for club address) and attractive sandy beach has become particularly popular with German visitors in recent years. Supermodel Claudia Schiffer is just one of the many Germans to own a luxury home here.

Sant Elm ★★

This peaceful holiday resort on the westernmost tip of Mallorca has a sandy beach and attractive harbour as well as several excellent seafood restaurants. The rocky islet of Sa Dragonera is just offshore. Once home to Redbeard the pirate, today it is better known for its variety of seabirds.

RESTAURANTS

Barlovento €€€ Top-notch fish restaurant with fantastic views. The menu varies depending on the daily catch. ⓐ Camí Vell des Far 1, Port d'Andratx ⓣ 971 67 10 49 ⓛ Open Tues–Sun 12.30–16.00 and 19.30–23.30

Bar Bellavista € The tapas, pizzas and filled rolls at this locals' bar make a pleasant snack lunch beside the old fishing harbour. ⓐ Avinguda Mateo Bosch 31, Port d'Andralx ⓣ 971 67 22 14 ⓛ Open 10.00–22.00

La Consigna € This popular cake shop and café serves filled croissants, meat pies and delicious almond cake to eat in or take away. *Ensaimadas*, the Mallorcan sugar-sprinkled spiral pastry, straight from the oven. Fresh bread available all day. ⓐ Carrer Mateo Bosch 19, Port d'Andratx ⓣ 971 67 16 04 ⓛ Open 10.00–19.00

Layn €€ A stylish harbourside restaurant with a good choice of meat and fish dishes. Try the gazpacho followed by spaghetti with prawns. Eat on the terrace or on the balcony overlooking the sea. ⓐ Carrer Almirante Riera Alemany 20, Port d'Andratx ⓣ 971 67 18 55 ⓦ www.layn.net ⓛ Open Tues–Sun 12.30–15.30 and 19.00–23.00

Na Caragola €€ A lively restaurant overlooking the island of Sa Dragonera, and serving superb paella and sangría. ⓐ Avinguda Rei Jaume I, Sant Elm ⓣ 971 23 90 06 ⓛ Open Thur–Tues 12.30–15.30 and 19.00–23.00

Rocamar €€€ Well-known for the excellence of its freshly-caught fish and shellfish. ⓐ Almirante Riera Alemany ⓣ 971 67 12 61 ⓛ Open Tues–Sun 12.30–16.00 and 19.00–23.00

During your stay enjoy alfresco dining

Cala Sant Vicenç
crystal-clear waters

Cala Sant Vicenç is one of the most perfect spots on the entire Mallorcan coast. Four small coves, each glistening with crystal-clear water, come together beneath the jagged ridge of Cavall Bernat, a magnificent limestone outcrop which casts its shadow into the sea. At night the water seems to turn pink in the setting sun. No wonder Cala Sant Vicenç has long been known as an artists' paradise.

THINGS TO SEE & DO

Cala Sant Vicenç Necropolis is a group of man-made caves used for burial purposes some 350 years ago. Signposted, on the right, driving into the Cala. A hike of around 45 minutes, beginning on the road above **Cala Carbó**, leads across wild countryside to the nearby resort of **Port de Pollença** (see page 40). Another good excursion is to take the bus into **Pollença** (see page 90) for the Sunday morning market.

BEACHES

The two largest coves, **Cala Barques** and **Cala Molins**, each have wide sandy beaches with sunbeds and sunshades for hire. At **Cala Molins** there are also concrete sunbathing platforms. The smaller beach at **Cala Clara** has fewer facilities, while **Cala Carbó** has excellent swimming and snorkelling but no sand. Swimming is safe throughout the resort, but currents can turn strong in stormy weather. Never swim beyond the rope across the entrance to the coves.

SHOPPING

On the main street, Carrer Temporal, you will find the **Gabriel Supermarket**. There's also **María**, a souvenir shop offering a wide selection of clothing, pottery, bags, shoes, buckets and spades.

RESTAURANTS & BARS

Cavall Bernat €€€ The top restaurant in the resort, serving 'new Mallorcan' dishes, such as quail stuffed with *foie gras*, duck breast with figs and grilled lobster in orange and cinnamon sauce. Expensive but worth it for that special night out. Ⓐ Carrer Temporal Ⓣ 971 53 02 50 Ⓛ Open 19.00–23.00; Sun and public holidays 13.00–15.00

Marisco €€ This is a new restaurant at the heart of the resort, specialising in fresh fish and seafood platters. Ⓐ Carrer de los Cala Molins Ⓛ Open 12.00–15.00 and 19.30–22.30

Pizzeria Cala Sant Vicenç €€ This family-orientated restaurant serves some of the best pizzas in Mallorca, home-made pasta dishes, nachos with mozzarella cheese and take-aways. Pavement terrace. Ⓐ Carrer Temporal Ⓣ 971 53 02 50 Ⓛ Open 13.00–15.00 and 19.00–23.00

Trotters Bar € All-day snacks including various delicious filled jacket potatoes, pies, baguettes and English bread sandwiches. Ⓐ Calle Temporal 31 Ⓛ Open 11.00–23.00 (summer only)

NIGHTLIFE

Two of the resort hotels, **Hotel Simar** and **Hotel Molins**, have free evening folk-dancing and flamenco shows. **Hotel Cala Sant Vicenç** has a piano bar and Spanish guitar music several times a week.

Beach at Cala Sant Vicenç

Port de Pollença
old-fashioned resort

With a horseshoe-shaped bay and a backdrop of craggy grey mountains, Port de Pollença is one of Mallorca's most attractive resorts. The safe, shallow water and golden sandy beaches make this an especially popular resort for families with young children. Those in search of a more active holiday will find sailing and windsurfing, as well as some excellent walks to nearby beaches and coves.

Visitors have been coming to Port de Pollença since the 1920s, and the hotels on the seafront have an old-fashioned air. The British crime writer Agatha Christie was one of the earliest visitors and she set one of her short stories in Pollença Bay. Fishing boats are moored beside luxury yachts, and there are numerous tiny beaches which are just the right size for a couple of families each.

Follow the Pine Walk, where pine trees lean into the sea and the waves lap almost at your feet, in the early evening, when everyone from young lovers to grandmothers come out in their best clothes to take part in the *paseo* (evening stroll). Afterwards you can watch the world go by with an apéritif at one of the cafés on the promenade.

SHOPPING

Aquamarine High-quality handmade jewellery in gold and silver. ⓐ Verge del Carme 15

Papelería Pizell Daily British newspapers, gifts and souvenirs. ⓐ Carrer Roger de Flor ⓣ 971 86 67 90

Maria's Just a few doors away, where you can hire a bicycle. ⓐ Carrer Roger de Flor ⓣ 971 86 43 36

THINGS TO SEE & DO

Bóquer Valley ★★

A walk of about an hour from Port de Pollença leads past the fortified Bóquer farmhouse across a rugged headland to the shingle beach at Cala Bóquer. On the way you might see wild goats, butterflies and birds, and several varieties of wild flowers. There are no facilities at Cala Bóquer, so take a picnic, plenty of water and sturdy shoes.

The harbour at Port de Pollença

Cap de Formentor ★★★
Buses and boat trips from Port de Pollença lead to this rocky cape, with stunning views of the wild north-eastern coast. Taxi boats run five times a day to Formentor beach, a beautiful white sandy beach on the edge of pine woods.

Sailing ★
Pollença Bay offers ideal conditions for sailing and windsurfing. **Sail and Surf** hires out sailboats and sailboards, and gives lessons to both beginners and the more advanced sailor. ⓐ Platja de la Gola ⓣ 971 86 53 46

BEACHES

The main beach at Port de Pollença stretches into the distance and gets less and less crowded as you move away from the resort towards Alcúdia. A regular bus service connects Port de Pollença with Mallorca's longest beach at Alcúdia (see page 44) and with the other resorts on the north-east coast.

RESTAURANTS & BARS

Bona Cepa €€ Mallorcan specialities including lobster casserole, fresh fish and *paellas*. ⓐ Carrer Juan Sebastián Elcano 3 ⓣ 971 86 50 04 Ⓛ Open Tues–Sun 12.30–15.30 and 19.00–23.00

The Codfather € Forgive the terrible pun: this British-owned restaurant serves some of the best fish and chips on Mallorca. Telephone your order in advance and it will be ready when you arrive, to eat in or take away. ⓐ Carrer Ecónom Torres 15 ⓣ 971 86 54 24 Ⓛ Open 09.30–23.00 (summer); 12.00–22.00 (winter)

Corb Marí € One of the best restaurants in town. Overlooking the sea in a pretty courtyard on the famous Pine Walk. Excellent Spanish cuisine and steaks, good value for money. ⓐ Carrer Formentor 72 ⓣ 971 86 70 40 Ⓛ Open Tues–Sun 13.00–15.00 and 19.00–23.00

La Lonja des Pescador €€€ The restaurant beside the yacht club on the harbour mole is the best place for a special evening out. Grilled fish and lobster are specialities and there is an interesting range of meat dishes. Moll Pesquer. 971 86 40 13 Open 12.00–16.00 and 19.30–23.00

Mulligan's Irish Pub € Irish and international drinks. Large terrace. Sandwiches/snacks served from 12.00–17.00. Live entertainers every Friday with Irish, pop, rock, blues, soul or jazz. Hums every evening. Atilio Boveri 5B, Port de Pollença 971 86 75 59 Open 10.30–04.00

El Posito € Really reasonable set menu at lunchtime with choice of tapas. Liebeig 8, Port de Pollença 971 86 54 13. Open 12.30–03.30, Sat 07.00–23.00

Na Ruixa €€ This elegant restaurant, set just back from the Pine Walk, is typical of the 'new Mallorcan' style of cooking, providing a fresh twist on traditional recipes. Carrer Mendez Nuñez 3 971 86 66 55 Open 13.00–14.00 and 19.00–23.00

Trotters Bar € Great breakfasts and evening meals, steaks, gammon, curries and pies. Carrer Temple Fielding 28, Port de Pollença 971 86 46 41 Open 11.00–01.00 (summer only)

NIGHTLIFE

Chivas The only disco in the resort, located near the market square, attracts a good mix of locals and tourists and features equally mixed dance music. Carrer Metge Llopis Open 23.00–06.00. Scratch and win cards for free drinks 23.00–01.00 Admission charge

Music Bar I Great atmosphere with music for relaxing, although it gets livelier as the night progresses. Carrer Méndez Núñez, esquina Roger de Flor Open Wed–Mon 13.30–04.00; closed Tues

Alcúdia
Mallorca's longest beach

The old town of Alcúdia and its port-resort of Port d'Alcúdia merge into each other at the northern tip of sweeping Alcúdia Bay. This is the start of the longest beach on Mallorca – with 10 km (6 miles) of golden sand gently shelving into the water, and sailing boats, sailboards and pedalos for hire, there is enough to keep everyone amused.

Alcúdia's old town

The old town itself has been tastefully restored in recent years. Nearly 2000 years ago this was the capital of Roman Mallorca; the remains of some Roman houses are still visible outside the town walls. The Moors built a new city on the site of the Roman town, and the medieval walls and gates were added after the Spanish conquest in 1229.

The heart of the old town, inside the walls, is now a pleasant pedestrian area of shady streets and ancient mansions, many of them converted into cafés and tapas bars. Get there by walking beneath the Portal del Moll, an ancient gateway from the port which is the symbol of Alcúdia. A lively market is held near here on Tuesday and Sunday mornings.

The easiest way to get to grips with the history of Alcúdia is to take a guided walking tour of the old town. The Tourist Office (971 89 26 15) organises a walk every Wednesday and Friday at 10.00. The tour starts outside the church and lasts about two hours. For an additional charge you can continue with a guided visit of the museum and Roman ruins.

THINGS TO SEE & DO

Hidropark ★★

With its giant water slides, swimming and boating pools, and three mini-golf courses in landscaped surroundings, this aquatic park makes a great day out for all the family. Ask your holiday rep for details of excursions.
Avinguda del Túcan 971 89 16 72 Open 10.30–18.00, May–Oct
Suitable for very young children

Roman Pollentia ★

There are few visible remains of the Roman city of Pollentia ('power'), perhaps because the islanders have recycled the building materials to create the present town. Signs point the way to the Teatre Romà, a well-preserved amphitheatre, and Ciutat Romà de Pollentia, where Roman houses can be seen. Both can be found off Avinguda de la Platja, just outside the medieval walls. The Tourist Office offers a walk through the Roman town every Wednesday and Friday at 10.00 (see Tip above).

SHOPPING

Alcúdia's Sunday market is a great place to pick up carved olive wood, local pottery and fine leather belts and bags.

BEACHES

The stretch from **Port d'Alcúdia** south to **Ca'n Picafort** is one enormous beach, with the kind of sand you dream about, washed by a clear blue sea. There are sunshades and sunbeds for hire, pedalos to play around in, and, if the beach gets too crowded, you can always find a quieter spot further along.

EXCURSION

A good excursion by hire car or bicycle is to follow the coast road north of Alcúdia, along the Cap d'es Pinar to the Ermita de la Victoria, a 17th-century hermitage. For an easier bike ride, take the road south of Alcúdia to reach the wetlands at S'Albufera, now a protected area (see page 48).

RESTAURANTS & BARS

Avinguda de Pere Mas i Reus, in the heart of the resort, is known by the locals as Dollar Street because of its many foreign restaurants and bars. Here you will find German beer gardens and English pubs, Chinese and Indian restaurants and even one or two Spanish bars.

Bogavante €€ This top-notch seafood restaurant is situated opposite the fishermen's pier with delightful views of the harbour. Stuffed mussels and mixed seafood grill are two of the house specialities. Ⓐ Carrer Teodor Canet 2 Ⓣ 971 54 73 64 Ⓒ Open Tues–Sun 13.00–16.00 and 19.00–23.00

Ca'n Moncho €€ Very popular restaurant serving steaks from Galicia, considered to be the best meat in Spain, mixed shellfish grill, fish dishes and tapas. ⓐ Calle Aucanada 1, Port d'Alcúdia ⓣ 971 54 87 55 ⓞ Open Tues–Sun 13.00–16.00 and 19.30–midnight

Cheers € This family-orientated bar and restaurant is named after the *Cheers* TV sitcom. It serves a large range of British and international beers, as well as other drinks, and the wide variety of food includes burgers, lasagne and Sunday lunch every day. Prices are reasonable and there is a special kids' menu. Entertainment is provided for children during the day, and for the whole family in the evening – with games, dancing and karaoke until 03.00. ⓐ Avinguda Venecia, off Avinguda de Pere Mas i Reus ⓣ 971 89 03 89 ⓞ Open 10.00–03.00

There is also a **Cheers 2** ⓐ Las Gaviotas, at the southern end of the resort at Calle Circuito del Lago ⓣ 971 89 26 58 ⓞ Open 10.00–01.30

Goodfellas € By contrast, children are definitely not welcome at this otherwise friendly music and internet café, which is a good pre-clubbing spot. There is live music several times a week and current video releases are also shown. ⓐ Carrer del Colomí, off Avinguda de Pere Mas i Reus

Khun Phanit's €€ This long-established Thai restaurant in the streets behind the harbour serves authentic Thai food at very reasonable prices. ⓐ Avinguda de la Platja 7 ⓣ 971 54 81 41 ⓞ Open 13.00–15.00 and 19.00–23.10, closed Mon lunch

NIGHTLIFE

Menta Alcúdia's biggest and most popular nightclub, modelled on a Roman temple, features an indoor heated swimming pool, plus two DJs and seven bars. The music is a mixture of Spanish and disco music, appealing to the trendily dressed 18–30 age group. The drinks are expensive but the club sandwiches are a must. ⓐ Avinguda Tucán, s/n ⓣ 971 89 19 72 ⓦ www.mentadisco.com ⓞ Open 22.00–06.00 ⓘ Admission charge

Ca'n Picafort
on sandy Alcúdia bay

Ca'n Picafort lies at the southern end of the long stretch of sandy beach that begins at Port d'Alcúdia. The attractive beachside promenade, lined with restaurants and bars, runs right through the resort as far as the marina and fishing harbour. From here it continues south along a rocky stretch of coast to a second beach known as Son Bauló.

THINGS TO SEE & DO

S'Albufera ★★

This wetland reserve between Ca'n Picafort and Port d'Alcúdia is an important breeding place for native and migratory birds, including ospreys, Montagu's harriers and Eleanora's falcons. A stroll along its numerous footpaths, with specially built bird hides in the marshes, makes a relaxing day out. You can hire binoculars at the reception centre. Cars are not allowed in the reserve and there is a walk of 1 km (1/2 mile) from the road. Cycling is allowed. Ⓐ The entrance is beside the Pont dels Anglesos on the main road to Port d'Alcúdia Ⓛ Open 09.00–dusk Ⓘ Admission free

Boating ★★

Glass-bottomed boat trips around Alcúdia Bay leave from beside the harbour.

Go-karting ★

For children aged from 4 years **Karting Ca'n Picafort** is a track in a complex that also has bars, eateries and a swimming pool. All gear is for hire. Ⓐ Poligono Industriel 13, carretera Alcudia-Artásh Ⓣ 971 85 12 82

Son Réal Necropolis ★

This prehistoric burial ground, dating from around 1000 BC, can be reached by a 20-minute walk from Son Bauló beach. Walk for another 15 minutes and you can swim out to the small island of Porros.

BEACHES

The main beach at **Ca'n Picafort** has all the facilities you could wish for, including water-skiing, pedalo hire and a windsurfing school. **Platja de Muro**, just north of the resort, is a quieter beach backed by tamarisk trees, sand dunes and the S'Albufera nature reserve.

RESTAURANTS & BARS

Ca'n Tomeu €€ A traditional family-orientated restaurant specialising in Mallorcan and Catalan cuisine. The tapas and the Mallorcan soup are highly recommended. ⓐ Carrer Ran de Mar 15 ⓣ 971 85 00 93 ◷ Open 13.00–15.00 and 19.00–22.00

Heladería San Remo € This large ice cream parlour also sells home-made cakes, strawberries and cream and freshly squeezed orange juice. ⓐ Passeig Enginyer Antoni Garau ◷ Open 10.00–01.00

Mandilego €€ A good place for that special night out – a traditional Spanish restaurant with a romantic atmosphere and paella to die for. ⓐ Carrer Isabel Garau 49 ⓣ 971 85 00 89 ◷ Open Tues–Sun 13.00–15.00 and 19.00–23.00

No 1 Pub €€ This British-owned pub has satellite TV and pool tables, lashings of pub grub and theme evenings. ⓐ Avinguda José Trias 4 ⓣ 971 85 06 95 ◷ Open 08.30–03.00

NIGHTLIFE

Charleys Western-themed nightclub. The drinks are expensive but admission is free. Basement disco. ⓐ Carrer Ran de Mar 15 (disco entrance at Carrer Platja 4) ⓣ 971 85 06 16 ◷ Open 19.00–04.00; disco open 23.00–05.00

Papaya This cocktail bar serves up many old favourites and a few strange mixtures of its own. Disco dancing most nights. ⓐ Passeig Colón 135 ⓣ 971 85 06 19 ⓦ www.papayadisco.com ◷ Open 20.00–06.00

Cala Rajada
delightful coast

Cala Rajada manages to be two things at once – a genuine fishing port, and a busy resort where water sports are the main attraction. This delightful stretch of coastline is studded with small coves, each with their own sandy beach.

THINGS TO SEE & DO

Hilltop sanctuary ★★

Take the bus from Cala Rajada to the delightful inland town of **Artà**, crowned by the hilltop sanctuary of Sant Salvador, which is reached by an avenue of cypress trees.

Cuevas d'Artà (Artà Caves) ★★

These magnificent underground rock formations lie a few kilometres south of Cala Rajada, close to the small resort of Canyamel. The one-hour guided tour comes complete with dazzling special effects. There are buses to the caves from Cala Rajada. ⓣ 971 84 12 93 ⓦ www.cuevasdarta.com ⓛ Open from 10.00; last visit 18.30 ⓘ Admission charge

The harbour at Cala Rajada

Jardins Casa March (Casa March Gardens) ★

The Mallorcan banker Joan March was a great collector of modern art and the gardens of his country home above the harbour have been turned into a sculpture park, with works by Rodin and Henry Moore among others. Visits by arrangement with the Tourist Office, Plaça dels Pins. 971 56 30 33

Punta de Capdepera ★★

A scenic 3 km (1½ mile) walk from the centre of the resort leads to the lighthouse at Punta de Capdepera – the easternmost point on Mallorca.

BEACHES

Font de Sa Cala, 5 km (3 miles) south of the resort, has clear water and gently shelving sand and is ideal for both swimming and sunbathing. Every kind of water sport is available here. **Son Moll**, the nearest beach to the centre, is popular with young families, while north of the resort are the attractive, quieter beaches of **Cala Guya**, **Cala Agulla** and **Cala Mesquida**.

RESTAURANTS

Ca'n Cardaix €€ Totally unpretentious and original. Bare floors, wooden benches, no tablecloths, no traffic, so the kids can run around while you eat good well-cooked food in peace. Av Canyamel, Font de Sa Cala 971 56 30 88 Open 09.00–late

Ses Rotges €€€ Michelin star. The top restaurant in the resort serves quality French cuisine in the back streets behind the port. Carrer Rafael Blanes 21 971 56 31 08 Open Mon, Wed and Fri–Sat 19.30–22.30 Reservations essential

NIGHTLIFE

Physical Smart but casual is the dress code at this popular disco aimed at anyone between 16 and 30. There is a laser show as well as regular foam parties and it is frequented by locals and visitors. Carrer Des Coconar Open 23.00–06.00 Admission charge

Cala Bona and Cala Millor
golden sands

Most of Mallorca's east coast is dotted with tiny creeks and coves, but at Cala Millor the golden sands just go on and on, stretching for more than 1 km (1/2 mile) along a wide, sheltered bay. The two resorts here – Cala Bona, the 'good bay', and Cala Millor, the 'better bay' – have almost merged into one mega-resort.

Cala Millor, with restaurants and bars lining its seafront promenade, is one long party in summer. Cala Bona, still based around its old fishing harbour, is a quieter resort with a smaller beach and a rather more laid-back atmosphere.

The best way to appreciate the feel of these two resorts is to walk from Cala Millor to Cala Bona in the early evening, along the seafront Passeig Marítim which connects the two, ending up at the harbour for a drink in one of the many waterside bars. Follow this with a seafood dinner at the port, and by the time you have walked back you will be ready to sample Cala Millor's nightlife.

 If you feel like a change from the beach, take the bus into the nearby town of Son Servera for the Friday morning market.

THINGS TO SEE & DO

Boat tours ★★

Glass-bottomed boats from Cala Millor tour the scenic east coast, north to Cala Rajada (page 50) and south to Porto Cristo (see page 58).

Fantasy Park ★

This outdoor play area near the centre of Cala Millor is paradise for children, with rides and inflatables for toddlers and older children alike. By the Parc de la Mar gardens Open 10.00–21.00

Pirate Ship ★★

Stops at Sa Coma, S'Illot, Porto Cristo and Cala Vaquace, which can only be reached by sea. Lunch on board. Cala Millor

Auto Safari-Zoo ★

See giraffes, zebra, elephants and monkeys at this miniature safari park between Cala Millor and Sa Coma. You can drive around the 4 km (2½ mile) circuit in your own car or take the zoo's mini-train. Get there from Cala Bona or Cala Millor on the Safari Bus (no charge) or the little road train (10.00–16.00). 971 81 09 09 Open 09.00–19.00; tiger shows 12.00, 14.00 and 15.30 Admission charge

Riding a buggy along the beach promenade

SHOPPING

Pastelería This baker's shop is highly recommended for its fresh bread, pastries and cakes. ⓐ Carrer dels Molins 3, Cala Millor

Torre de n'Amer (n'Amer Tower) ★★

You can walk up to this medieval watchtower on the headland of Punta de n'Amer, with spectacular views out to sea and back down over the resort. The walk takes around 45 minutes and there is a bar at the top selling drinks and snacks. ⓐ Between Cala Millor and Sa Coma

BEACHES

The beach at **Cala Millor** has clear water, gently sloping sand, sunshades and sunbeds for hire and water sports facilities. You can touch the bottom up to 100 m (330 ft) out. **Cala Bona**'s cove-like beach is smaller, but with similar facilities. Seaweed can be a problem here.

RESTAURANTS & BARS

L'Angolo € This typical Italian restaurant with a shady outdoor terrace serves popular staples, such as pizza and lasagne, but the house speciality is breaded veal escalope. ⓐ Carrer Binicanella 18C, Cala Millor ⓣ 971 81 35 76 ⓛ Open 11.30–16.00 and 18.30–midnight

Bar Nàutic € This café-bar overlooking Cala Bona's port attracts locals as well as visitors and serves snacks such as hamburgers, rolls and *pa amb oli* (see page 95) ⓐ Avinguda de n'Antoni Garau 21, Cala Bona ⓣ 971 58 60 27 ⓛ Open Mon–Sat 08.00–03.00, Sun 10.00–late

Bon Gust €€ Specialises in Mediterranean Mallorquín cuisine, fresh fish and paella. They also serve a *fideau paella* (with pasta instead of rice) and a variety of pasta dishes. The menu includes tapas and many other interesting dishes, all at reasonable prices.

ⓐ Carrer Es Rafal 3, Cala Millor ⓣ 971 58 59 30 ⓛ Open Tues–Sun 12.00–16.00 and 19.00–midnight

Ca's Candil €€ An excellent Spanish grill-restaurant with a covered outdoor terrace. The barbecued meat dishes, such as pork steaks and chicken breasts, are recommended but paella and lobster are also available, along with a good range of Spanish tapas. ⓐ Carrer Fetget 3, Cala Millor ⓣ 971 58 50 34 ⓛ Open 19.00–23.00

El Pescador €€ This relatively formal Spanish restaurant beside the port specialises in seafood but has meat dishes as well. The paella and the grilled salmon are highly recommended. ⓐ Port de Cala Bona ⓣ 971 58 66 02 ⓛ Open Tues–Sun 12.00–15.00 and 18.00–23.00

Saddancers € A lively bar that is a great place for families, with activities and entertainment every night. The list extends to sporting events, bingo, quizzes and karaoke, and there is an extensive play area and a cinema for the kids. ⓐ Carrer de Na Llambies 81, Cala Bona ⓣ 971 58 72 43 ⓛ Open 12.00–16.00 and 20.00–late

Son Floriana €€€ This Mallorcan country house in the quiet back roads of Cala Bona is known for its excellent cuisine. The atmosphere is formal but friendly, and you can eat in the house, decorated with works of art, or in the beautiful gardens. Specialities include mixed paella and châteaubriand steak, and the wine cellar has a fine selection of Mallorcan and Spanish wines. ⓐ Avinguda de Las Magnòlia, Cala Bona ⓣ 971 58 60 75 ⓛ Open 13.00–15.00 and 19.00–midnight

NIGHTLIFE

With its low-key nightlife, Cala Bona is not for the clubbers of this world but there are plenty of bars to choose from in the harbour area, some with live music. A 20-minute walk will take you to vibrant Cala Millor, lined with bars and clubs.

Sa Coma and S'Illot
relaxing resorts

These two resorts, each with their own sandy beach, are separated by a small rocky headland. The resorts have everything you need for a relaxing family holiday – and when you feel like a change of scenery, you can simply hop on a boat for a trip up the east coast, or take the Badia Express road train which links the resorts with Cala Millor.

THINGS TO SEE & DO

Golf ★

Children will happily spend all day at **Golf Paradis**, a 54-hole mini-golf course, set in a make-believe landscape with waterfalls, palm trees, lakes and a windmill. The course is also open in the evenings, when you play under floodlights. ⓐ Carrer las Lilas, s/n, off Avinguda de les Palmeres ⓣ 971 81 10 02 ◷ Open 10.00–22.00

Auto Safari-Zoo ★

See giraffes, zebra, elephants and monkeys at this miniature safari park, on the road between Sa Coma and Cala Millor. You can get there from Sa Coma and S'Illot on the free Safari Bus (see page 53 for more details). ⓣ 971 81 09 09 ◷ Open 09.00–19.00 ⓘ Admission charge

Torre de n'Amer (n'Amer Tower) ★★

It takes around 45 minutes to walk up to this medieval watchtower and enjoy its spectcular views. There is a bar at the top selling drinks and snacks (see page 54 for more details).

SHOPPING

The **Caprabo** hypermarket on Avinguda de les Palmeres is a good place to stock up on food, including fresh seafood.

RESTAURANTS

BiBaBo € Families are welcome at this very good value café and music bar on the seafront promenade. The food is a mixture of Spanish and British, with dishes such as mussels *marinera* or chicken and chips. Ⓐ Passeig Neptú 11, S'Illot Ⓣ 971 81 01 60 Ⓛ Open 08.30–23.00

Surfers on the beach

Es Cuerot €€ A cellar restaurant serving traditional Mallorcan cuisine, such as paella, stuffed squid and tapas. The *frito mallorquín*, a fry-up of lamb and vegetables, is a speciality here. You can eat out of doors on the terrace, or downstairs in the restaurant. Ⓐ Carrer Dàlies, Sa Coma Ⓣ 971 81 02 80 Ⓛ Open 09.00–16.00 and 18.00–midnight

Lago €€€ A top-notch restaurant serving Spanish and Mallorcan cuisine – just the place for a celebration. The mixed seafood platter and fillet steak in Roquefort sauce are both highly recommended. Prices are above average but worth it. For a cheaper meal you can eat in the same owners' tapas bar next door. Ⓐ Carrer Mitjorn 9, S'Illot Ⓣ 971 81 02 09 Ⓛ Open 12.30–15.30 and 19.00–23.30

NIGHTLIFE

Crazy Monkeys Music bar with a monkey theme and a laid-back atmosphere. Spanish-style cocktail bar. Ⓐ Rosa dels Vents, S'Illot Ⓛ Happy Hour 20.00–23.00 and midnight–02.00

Espace Don't get left behind in the rush for the only disco in Sa Coma and S'Illot. The dress code is casual and there is a mixed Spanish and tourist clientele. Ⓐ Carrer Rosa dels Vents, S'Illot Ⓛ Open 22.00–06.00

Porto Cristo
family resort

With a wide sandy beach at the end of a long curving bay, Porto Cristo is many people's favourite spot on Mallorca's east coast. Sailors are drawn here by its calm, sheltered waters, and the marina beside the beach is a good place for spotting luxury yachts. It has some of Mallorca's leading family attractions, including the Coves del Drac. There is not an extensive range of shops or restaurants but this is a characterful resort ideal for older holidaymakers and small children.

THINGS TO SEE & DO

Coves del Drac (Dragon Caves) ★★★

A trip to these caves is one of the highlights of any holiday on Mallorca – but don't go if you are claustrophobic. You walk along 2 km (1½ miles) of paths inside vast underground caverns, gazing at stalactites that have formed over the centuries into eerie shapes. The caves are illuminated and the icing on the cake is a concert of classical music as you ride on a boat across Lake Martel, Europe's largest underground lake. Book through your holiday rep. Ⓐ Just outside Porto Cristo on the road to Cales de Mallorca Ⓣ 971 82 07 53 Ⓒ Open 10.00–17.00 (Apr–Oct), 10.45–noon and 14.00–15.30 (Nov–Mar) (tours on the hour) ❶ Admission charge

Coves dels Hams (Caves of Hams) ★

If you've enjoyed the Coves del Drac, you could visit these caves too. Just outside Porto Cristo, they are not as big (or as popular) as the Coves del Drac. Ⓐ On the road to Manacor Ⓣ 971 82 09 88 Ⓒ Open 10.00–18.00 (Mar–Oct), 10.30–17.30 (Nov–Feb) ❶ Admission charge

Mallorca Aquarium ★

A small aquarium, with exotic fish from around the world, including piranhas, poisonous puffer fish and electric eels. Ⓐ Carrer de la Vela, near the Coves del Drac Ⓣ 971 82 09 71 Ⓒ Open 09.30–7.00 (Apr–Oct), 11.00–15.00 (Nov–Mar) ❶ Admission charge

Beach at Porto Cristo

RESTAURANTS

Cap d'es Toi €€ This popular restaurant specialises in fresh fish and meat dishes. There is a choice of nearly 20 home-made pizzas and 50 varieties of *pa amb oli* (see page 95). Passeig es Riuet s/n Porto Cristo 971 82 25 78 Open 12.00–23.00 (Feb–Oct)

Club Náutico €€ This seafood restaurant has a prime position overlooking the marina. Prices are expensive but affordable, making it the best place in the resort for a special treat. The house speciality is paella. Carrer de la Vela 29 971 82 02 99 Open 12.00–14.30 and 19.30–23.00

Golden Bay € Located alongside the rivulet running into Porto Cristo Bay, this is a delightful spot to relax overlooking the water, watching the small boats plying back and forth. Cantonese and Shanghai cooking, with a set menu and daily special. Carrer Paseo Rivet 25, Porto Cristo 971 82 25 05 Open 11.00–16.00 and 18.00–midnight

Sa Gruta Nova €€ Located in an old country house, with a delightful Mallorcan courtyard surrounded by ancient trees. Mallorcan and Mediterranean cooking with an emphasis on rice dishes. Vegetarian menu. Carretera Porto Cristo – Cala Millor Km 2.6, Porto Cristo 971 82 09 43 Open Mar–Oct 19.00–23.00

Boats at Cales de Mallorca

Cales de Mallorca
beaches and bays

Cales de Mallorca is the collective name for around 20 small coves that dot the coastline between Porto Cristo and Porto Colom. Many of them can only be reached by boat, but three of the larger coves form the setting for a small, self-contained resort – also known as Cales de Mallorca. This resort is very child-orientated, with lots for children to do.

Each of the three bays – Cala Antena, Cala Domingos Grans and Cala Domingos Petits – have their own sandy beaches. Loungers and sunshades are for hire in Cala Domingos Grans and Cala Domingos Petits. At the largest beach, Cala Domingos Grans, it is also possible to hire pedalos. The Calas Express road train trundles between the beaches, but if you are feeling energetic you should take the coastal path for its

SHOPPING

The shops are concentrated at the Centro Comercial. Try **Carolyn** for jewellery, including Majorica pearls, **Euro-Perfumería Eden** for duty-free perfumes and **Casa Pila Sports** for sports gear and swimwear. For local arts and crafts, head into nearby **Felanitx** for its busy Sunday morning market, when heavy brown-glazed pottery is displayed on the church steps. This is a good place to buy ceramics and enamelled goods.

stunning clifftop views – especially at dawn. Most of the action 'down-town', including shops and restaurants, is found in the Centro Comercial, a shopping centre with a mini-golf course and sandy play area at its centre.

Hire a bike to explore the surrounding countryside, including the inland town of Felanitx and the charming fishing port of Porto Colom. Serious cyclists can even tackle the climb to the sanctuary of San Salvador above Felanitx.

THINGS TO SEE & DO

Boat trips ★★

A glass-bottomed boat trip along the fjord-like east coast, with its secluded beaches and pine-fringed coves, is a must. Some of the trips stop at Porto Cristo, giving you time to visit the Coves del Drac (Dragon Caves, see page 58). Others visit the pretty sand and shingle beach at Cala Murada, just south of Cales de Mallorca.

Tropical gardens ★

A tropical garden and banana plantation, in **Jumaica** you will find birds flying free, pools, cascades and a restaurant/bar (€). Ⓐ Carretera Porto Colom–Porto Cristo, Km 4.5 Ⓣ 971 83 33 55 Ⓦ www.jumaicapark.com Ⓛ Open 09.00–18.00(summer); 10.00–16.30 (winter). Restaurant closed Mon Ⓘ Admission charge

RESTAURANTS & BARS

Bar Mallorca €€ This Spanish bar serves paella, pizzas and pasta dishes on a covered patio. The crazy golf course outside is operated by the bar, so you can watch your children play while you tuck in. Ⓐ Centro Comercial Ⓣ 971 83 32 17 Ⓛ Open 09.00–23.30

Ca'n Pep Noguera €€ Classic Mallorcan cooking in a romantic setting, just outside the resort. House specialities include 'dirty rice', a Mallorcan version of paella. Ⓐ Carretera Porto Cristo– Porto Colom Ⓣ 971 83 33 55 Ⓛ Open Tues–Sun 12.30–16.00 and 19.00–23.00

Casa Pila €€ This is a typically British joint serving English breakfast, roast dinner and home-made pies. ⓐ Centro Comercial ⓣ 609 13 66 23 ⓛ Open Tues–Sun 09.00–15.00 and 18.30–22.30

Chaplin €€ Fresh fish is the speciality at this relaxed and friendly Spanish-style restaurant in the centre of the resort. ⓐ Centro Comercial ⓣ 971 83 41 65 ⓛ Open 09.30–16.00 and 17.00–23.00

La Macarena € A friendly Spanish bar overlooking the children's playground, with a good selection of traditional tapas. ⓐ Centro Comercial ⓣ 971 83 32 34 ⓛ Open 10.00–01.00

Mar Azul € This café, with live music three times a week, serves simple, good-value meals. ⓐ Carrer J&M Caballero 6 ⓣ 971 83 32 10 ⓛ Open 09.00–15.30 and 18.00–22.30

Marítimo € This restaurant overlooking the beach at Cala Domingo Gran has a water-slide, a children's playground and pool, and meals ranging from paella to grilled sole and chips. ⓐ Platja Domingos Grans ⓛ Open 10.00–18.00

Maysi €€ Roast lamb and grilled prawns are two of the specialities at this good-value restaurant. You dine on a covered patio with sea views. ⓐ Centro Comercial ⓣ 971 88 33 43 ⓛ Open 11.30–23.00

Oriente City €€ This Chinese restaurant serves classic Cantonese cooking, such as sweet and sour chicken and beef in oyster sauce, on a shady terrace in a quiet back street. ⓐ Carrer Cala Romaguera ⓣ 971 83 41 67 ⓛ Open 12.30–16.00 and 18.30–midnight

Pizzeria d'Alfil €€ A very popular friendly, family-orientated restaurant serving pizzas, pasta and cocktails on an outdoor terrace with a fountain. There is live music plus a DJ or entertainer here most nights. ⓐ Centro Comercial ⓣ 971 83 40 88 ⓛ Open 11.00–04.00

Sol y Vida €€ Overlooking Cala Domingo Bay, this air-conditioned restaurant is the ideal place to sample traditional Basque and Spanish food. The Pub **La Cuava** is a small intimate bar with an outside terrace, located on the cliff top with sweeping sea views where you can eat or sit and have a drink at any time of day. At **La Musica Bar** you can dance the night away until 05.00 or relax on the terrace.
ⓐ Manzana F37 Cala Murada ⓣ 971 83 31 70 Open 11.00–midnight

NIGHTLIFE

The resort's main square is the place to be at night, with pavement artists, buskers and hair-braiders in the street and plenty of entertainment in the bars around it.

Flamingos This bar caters to all tastes in music and has a satellite TV and a pool table. ⓐ Carrer Cala Romanguera Open 19.00–late; Happy Hour 22.00–01.00

Jupiter It's mostly British dance music at this lively bar-disco, which only really gets into full swing after midnight. Children welcome. ⓐ Carrer Cala Romaguera Open 20.00–03.00; Happy Hour 16.00–midnight

Rock Cola This is the largest bar in town. Special barbecues, ice creams and Rock Cola cocktails. Party atmosphere. Live entertainment every evening followed by disco, with the only international top professional DJ in the resort. ⓐ Cales de Mallorca ⓣ 650 43 38 78 Open May–Oct 16.00–04.00; Happy Hour 20.00–01.00

Le Saint Louis Serves great cocktails and has an incredible atmosphere at night. ⓐ Centro Comercial Open 18.00–late

Tiffany's There's a varied mix of music styles to suit the international clientele of this nightclub. The age group ranges from 20 to 40 (under-18s not allowed) and there is no specific dress code. ⓐ Carrer Cala Romaguera Open midnight–06.00

Porto Colom
tranquil fishing village

The fishing village of Porto Colom was named in honour of Christopher Columbus who, it is said, was born here. Set around a deep, natural harbour, the resort still has the feel of a small fishing port and is popular with Mallorcan and Spanish visitors. It is ideal for a peaceful, relaxing holiday and a great centre for families with young children.

Porto Colom was once the port for the nearby town of Felanitx, and thrived by exporting Mallorcan wine to France. However, when phylloxera (a kind of insect) killed the island's vineyards, its role as a port diminished. It has only recently discovered a new life as a tourist resort. Thankfully, it has retained much of its old charm by restricting the number of hotels and preserving the fishing harbour.

Porto Colom is the ideal setting for all water sports and the best beach is located 2 km (1½ miles) to the south, in the quiet resort of **Cala Marçal**. Should you tire of the seaside, keen walkers will enjoy exploring the Serra de Llevant mountain range, with its spectacular views out to sea and over the Plain of Mallorca. Its highest points are crowned by the 14th-century **Ermita de Sant Salvador** (Hermitage of Saint Salvador) and the ancient **Castel de Santueri** (Castle of Sanctuary), built originally as a defence against pirates and corsairs.

THINGS TO SEE & DO

Boat trips ★★

Exploring the Porto Colom coastline aboard a glass-bottomed boat is always a fun day out for all the family.

Golf ★

In the hills just a short distance from the resort, the challenging 18-hole **Vall d'Or** golf course has spectacular views from the fairways and welcome sea breezes in summer. ⓐ Carretera Porto Colom–Cala d'Or, Km 7,7 ⓣ 971 83 70 01 ⓛ Open all year

Horse riding ★
Spend a splendid day on horseback, trekking in the countryside around Portocolom. You can even ride to the Consolacíon Sanctuary or visit a castle for lunch. ⓐ Escola d'Equitació Son Menut, Camí de Son Negre, Felanitx ⓣ 971 58 29 20

RESTAURANTS & BARS

Bar Club Nàutic Bona Pesca € A real locals' bar, right on the water's edge. ⓐ Carrer des Pescadors ⓣ 971 82 46 90

Bob's Restaurant € Home-made food such as lasagne, plus all-day English breakfasts, pies, grills and steaks. Live music Tues, Fri and Sun nights. ⓐ C'as Corsa 15 ◷ Open 09.00–15.00 and 18.00–02.00

Ca'n Tia €€ This popular family restaurant serves international and Mallorcan dishes. ⓐ Carrer de Cala Marçal 2 ⓣ 971 82 55 96 ◷ Open 13.00–15.00 and 19.00–22.00; closed Sat lunch

Mar Blau €€ Stunning terrace views. Serves good food with a difference and has an extensive wine list. Children welcome. ⓐ Av. Cala Marçal 1, Porto Colom ⓣ 971 82 49 15 ◷ Open 18.00–late

Restaurante Chino Shanghai €€ Hard to miss with its red and green pagoda frontage! Over one hundred dishes to choose from. Try its Chinese fondue. Eat in or take away. ⓐ Asunción 8 ⓣ 971 82 43 53 ◷ Open 12.00–16.00 and 18.00–23.30

NIGHTLIFE

Bocachica Caribbean cocktails, live music and entertainment. ⓐ Avenida Cala Marçal ◷ Open 08.00–late

Calipso Porto Colom's only disco attracts a young crowd, eager to party. ⓐ Carrer d'Hernán Cortés ◷ Open 23.00–06.00

Pay-pay There's often live music outside this popular Polynesian-style cocktail bar. ⓐ Plaça Corsa ◷ Open 17.00–03.00

The village of Cala Figuera

Cala d'Or
celebrity hide-out

This chic resort, where white, flat-roofed villas surround the former fishing harbour, has grown over the years to embrace several of the nearby creeks and coves. At the heart of the resort is the marina, a good place for spotting luxury yachts and perhaps catching a glimpse of a celebrity owner drinking at one of the waterside bars.

The central resort of Cala d'Or is one of the liveliest on the east coast, with most of the action taking place in and around the marina, or in the downtown area between the marina and the beach. To the north and south stretch a succession of rocky coves, where small resorts have gradually grown up around fine sandy beaches. To the north is Cala Serena, to the south, Cala Egos, Cala Barca and the fishing village of Porto Petro. Cala Mondragó, south of Cala d'Or, has twin beaches connected by a clifftop path on the edge of a nature reserve. You can travel between all of these coves on the Cala d'Or Express, a mini-train which trundles back and forth between Cala Serena and Cala Mondragó in summer.

Take a trip on a glass-bottomed boat to see all of Cala d'Or's coves in one go – then decide which one you would like to go back to for an afternoon on the beach.

BEACHES

Cala Gran, close to the centre of the resort, is the largest beach. Near here is **Cala d'Or** itself, a pine-fringed cove with a small but crowded white-sand beach. Sunbeds, sunshades and pedalos can be hired at both of these beaches, and also at **Cala Mondragó**, **Cala Egos** and **Cala Barca**.

EXCURSIONS

Cala Figuera ★★★

This charming village, a few kilometres south of Cala d'Or, is still very much a fishing port, with fishermen's cottages lining the narrow inlet. There are several arts and crafts shops in the village as well as some excellent seafood restaurants. Although there is no beach here, there are good ones nearby at Cala Mondragó Nature Park and Cala Santanyí.

Es Trenc ★★

If Cala d'Or's beaches get too crowded, take the morning bus to Es Trenc. This is a protected area where no development is allowed. The beautiful beach of clear blue water and golden sand, backed by pine trees and dunes, stretches for almost 5 km (3 miles) along the south-eastern shore. There is a small bar-restaurant here and you can hire sunshades, but there are few other facilities. Be aware, though, that Es Trenc is popular with nudists, although they tend to gather at one end of the beach.

Portopetro ★★

In contrast to lively Cala d'Or, the neighbouring fishing village of Portopetro, just a short distance along the coast, has retained its old-world character, with its traditional fishing boats, picturesque port and charming whitewashed fishermen's cottages.

Sa Colònia de Sant Jordi ★★

Once the haunt of pirates and smugglers, this is one of Mallorca's quieter seaside resorts, with a pocket-handkerchief-sized beach. There are also daily boat trips at 09.30 from Sa Colònia's port to the island of Cabrera – a protected National Land-Sea Park.

RESTAURANTS & BARS

Blanco y Negro €€ Popular seafood restaurant by the marina. Marina de Cala d'Or 971 64 34 65 Open noon–midnight

Bona Taula €€€ Intimate and elegant for a special occasion. Mallorcan dishes. Rafael Adrover 32, Cala d'Or 971 16 71 47 Open Wed–Mon 19.00–23.00

Café Bon Bar € Great for coffee, a drink or a snack on a well-placed terrace, high above the fishing harbour. Carrer Virgen del Carmen 27, Cala Figuera 971 64 52 06 Open 11.00–midnight

Cala €€ Excellent fish restaurant. Carrer Virgen del Carmen, Cala Figuera 971 64 50 18 Open 08.00–01.00

Ca'n Trompé €€ Hugely popular Mallorcan restaurant that serves an excellent-value three-course menu. Av. de Bélgica 12, Cala d'Or 971 65 73 41 Open 12.30–15.30 and 19.00–23.30

Don Leone €€ Pizzas and pasta dishes are freshly made to order at this Italian-style grill with a shady terrace. Carrer Toni Costa 13, Cala d'Or 971 64 34 14 Open 12.00–midnight

The Dumpling €€ Friendly, family-run restaurant serving Irish beef and Guiness pie or beef and ale pie. Carrer Toni Costa 5, Cala d'Or 971 65 70 40 Open Thur–Tues 10.30–23.30

SHOPPING

The Sunday morning market in the nearby town of **Felanitx** is one of the best in Mallorca and well worth a visit. This is a good place to pick up some local pottery. Visit **Cala Figuera** for interesting souvenirs, including pottery, glass and Lladró sculptures.

El Lazo €€ The mixed grill is highly recommended at this meat-oriented Spanish restaurant. There's a big menu for kids and the prices are reasonable. Carrer Toni Costa 23, Cala d'Or 971 65 74 38 Open 12.00–15.00 and 18.00–23.00

Lineker's Bar € Has loads of TVs for watching football. Fantastic atmosphere at night and very friendly staff. Toni Costa 43, Cala d'Or 971 32 36 51 www.linekers-bar.com Open 12.00–13.00 Apr–Oct

Pavarotti €-€€ Italian cooking with the emphasis on fresh produce. Carrer Cristofor Colom 99, Porto Petro 971 65 81 71 Open 12.00–15.00, 18.00–midnight, closed Tues lunch and Sat lunch

Porto Petro €€ One of the port's top fish restaurants, with fantastic views over the fishing harbour. Passeig d'es Port 49, Porto Petro 971 65 77 04 Open 11.30–16.00 and 18.30–23.00

Port Petit €€€ This upmarket restaurant overlooking the marina specialises in seafood, including Mediterranean rock lobster. Marina de Cala d'Or 971 64 30 39 Open 18.30–23.00

NIGHTLIFE

Chic Palace Charts and house music for 20-somethings. Plaça Costa 1, Cala d'Or 971 65 97 94 Open 23.00–07.00 Admission charge

Club Passion Electric atmosphere. 'Anything goes' attitude positively encouraged. Carrer S'Espalmador 3, Cala d'Or Open 22.00–late

Cotton Club Top rock, Latin and disco (no house) and special VIP lounge. Edificio del Pueblo, Cala D'Or 699 76 25 25 Open 21.00–06.00

La Cueva Tiny disco-pub set in cave-like surroundings in sleepy Porto Petro. Passeig d'es Port 51, Porto Petro Open 22.30–02.00

Mondbar Superb cocktails and a fantastic open-air dance floor. Carrer Pintor Bernareggi, Cala Figuera Open 20.30–late

Pinte A popular pint-sized jazz bar. Carrer Pintor Bernareggi, Cala Figuera Open 19.30–03.00

S'Arenal
Palma's golden beach

The bustling resort of S'Arenal sits at one end of the long Platja de Palma, more than 5 km (3 miles) of wide sandy beach, with the twin resort of Ca'n Pastilla at the other end. The resorts have a highly international flavour, with English pubs, German and Dutch bars.

There is plenty in S'Arenal to keep everyone amused, with facilities for windsurfing and water-skiing as well as pedalo hire. Children can splash safely around in the shallow water, and there are also a number of playgrounds. A palm-lined promenade runs the length of the resort, offering good views across Palma Bay; if you don't feel like walking, take the mini-train or go for a ride in a *galera* (horse and carriage).

THINGS TO SEE & DO

Aqualand ★★

Billed as the largest water park in Europe, Aqualand has enough thrills and spills to keep children busy all day. One of the rides is called the Black Hole and another Kamikaze, though there are more sedate rides. It's a great day out for all the family, with go-karting, parrot shows and a mini-farm. ⓐ Beside Palma–S'Arenal motorway, exit 13 (15 minutes' walk from S'Arenal) ⓣ 971 44 00 00 ⓛ Open 10.00–18.00 (Jul/Aug); 10.00–17.00 (May, June & Sept); closed Oct–Apr ⓘ Admission charge (free for under-3s)

Golf Fantasia ★

Play fantasy golf at three 18-hole putting courses in a landscape of caves waterfalls and tropical gardens with dinosaurs. ⓐ Carretera del Arenal 56 (between Balneario 4 and 5) ⓣ 971 74 33 34 ⓛ Open 09.00–late

RESTAURANTS & BARS

Beachcombers € Run by Canadians, this friendly basement bar-café has a breezy, international style appealing to visitors of all ages. ⓐ Carrer Trasimeno 41 ⓣ 971 26 66 60 ⓛ Open 10.30–late

Can Torrat €€ An open-air ranch-style restaurant popular with Mallorcans who head here at weekends for platefuls of barbecued meat. Camí de las Meravelles 971 26 20 55 Open 13.00–03.00

Ca's Cotxer €€ Generous portions of Mallorcan classics, with an emphasis on fresh fish and seafood. Carretera del Arenal 31 971 26 20 49 Open Tues–Sun 11.30–16.00 and 19.00–23.30

China Ming € This is the best and most authentic of the Chinese restaurants in S'Arenal – the set daytime menus are very good value. Carrer Berlin 5 971 49 28 78 Open 12.00–16.00 and 19.00–midnight

Coach and Horses € You won't get much more British than this local. It's a friendly place with music, serving pies, pasties, local wines and imported beers and ciders as well as sangría. Carrer San Bartolome 9 971 44 26 21 Open 10.00–14.00 and 19.00–late

Moli de Can Pere €€€ Converted 1631 mill with rustic tables in delightful courtyard. Specialities include rabbit, suckling pig and lamb. Carrer S'Arenal-Llucmajor Open 13.00–16.00 and 19.30–20.00

El Puerto € Overlooking the sea with a shady terrace, the restaurant's speciality is shellfish and grills, but they do great sandwiches. Carrer Costa i Llobera 971 44 04 67 Open Wed–Mon 19.00–late

NIGHTLIFE

S'Arenal is one of the wildest spots for partying.

RIU-Palace One of Mallorca's top nightspots, with room for 2000 people in a giant disco popular with young locals and visitors alike. Techno/chart music, go-go dancers, laser show. Carrer del Llaut Open 22.00–06.00

Zorba's An international disco with a youngish clientele. Dance/house music, two stages, 11 bars and room for 4000 people! The locals flock here at weekends too. Dress as you feel and don't forget – you pay on leaving here. Avinguda de Son Rigo Open 22.00–06.00

Ca'n Pastilla & Playa de Palma

Just five minutes from Palma de Mallorca, these two resorts smoothly blend into one another as you stroll along the main promenade. Ideal for families young and old, days are spent lazing on the 7 km (4 miles) beach or taking part in the many water sports on offer. At night, choose between living it up in one of the many bars and discos or enjoying a quiet meal on the seafront overlooking the beautiful bay of Palma.

RESTAURANTS & BARS

Chon Pra-Pa €€ Authentic Thai restaurant with ingredients delivered from Thailand. ⓐ Carrer Palangres 9, Ca'n Pastilla ⓣ 971 74 53 44 ◷ Open 12.00–16.00 and 18.00–midnight

Manchester Pub € Always a favourite with visitors, especially sports enthusiasts for its extra large screen. ⓐ Carrer de Gregal, Ca'n Pastilla ⓣ 971 26 25 97 ◷ Open Mon–Sat 11.00–16.00 and 20.00–01.00

El Rancho Picadero €€ Not for vegetarians. Meat grilled over a wood fire and served on a beautiful garden terrace. ⓐ Carrer del Flamenco, Ca'n Pastilla ⓣ 971 26 10 02 ◷ Open noon–midnight

Ricky's Tavern € Good British grub including full breakfasts and home-made specialities, plus nightly quizzes and a karaoke night. ⓐ Avinguda Bartolome Riutort ◷ Open 10.30–15.00 and 20.00–01.00

NIGHTLIFE

The Joy Palace Promotional nights and top name 'Euro DJs'. ⓐ Carrer de la Missio de San Gabriel, Playa de Palma ◷ Open 22.00–06.00
Buskers Not-to-be missed. Jam sesssions with professional entertainers. Buskers during day. ⓐ Carrer Bellamar ◷ Open all day until late
Rising Sun Live music bar run by a member of the Drifters. Sunday nights for soul jam-sessions. ⓐ Carrer Virgili 4, C'an Pastilla ◷ Open 22.00–until late (See also Nightlife section on previous page)

EXCURSIONS
Out & about

Valldemossa
celebrity village

Valldemossa (pronounced 'Val-de-*moss*-er') is one of the best-known mountain villages in Mallorca. Here Frédéric Chopin and his mistress George Sand (real name Aurore Dudevant) spent the winter of 1838–39 in the Reial Cartoixa (or Charterhouse). The monastery and scenery have changed little since, and Valldemossa remains well worth visiting, if only for the monastic peace after the bustle of Mallorca's beach resorts.

Chopin and the French novelist George Sand came to Mallorca to escape the gossip of Paris, and in the hope that the mild climate would improve Chopin's health. However, Chopin's piano failed to arrive, his health deteriorated and so did their relationship. Afterwards, Sand wrote an angry book in which she described the Mallorcans as 'thieves and monkeys'.

Valldemossa is also the birthplace of the island's patron saint, Santa Catalina Thomás, and nearly every house in the village has a painted tile beside the front door asking for the saint's protection.

SHOPPING

Valldemossa boasts plenty of small arts and handicraft shops, such as **Es Teix**, **Capamunta** and **Giravent**, selling fine hand-made pottery, glass, jewellery, woodwork and table linen from all over the island.

Souvenirs Catalina Calafat This jam-packed shop sells everything from Lladró, lace and leatherware to *siurells* (clay whistles) and replica Chopin pianos. ⓐ Plaça Cartoixa 1, Valldemossa ⓣ 971 61 24 61 ◔ Open 10.00–19.00

◑ *Valldemossa has changed little over the years*

THINGS TO SEE & DO

Charterhouse ★★

Visit the Charterhouse monastery to see the monk's cell where Frédéric Chopin and George Sand stayed, as well as the old pharmacy and an excellent museum of modern art including work by Picasso and Miró. There are regular recitals of Chopin's music and you can even buy a copy of Sand's book. ⓣ 971 61 21 06 Ⓛ Open Mon–Sat 09.30–18.00, Sun 10.00–13.00 ⓘ Admission charge

---

Don't leave Valldemossa without trying the local delicacies – *coca de patates* (light, fluffy buns dusted in icing sugar) – washed down with a chilled *horchata de almendra* (almond milkshake).

La Granja ★★★

One of Mallorca's finest country houses has been turned into a fascinating open-air museum of rural life and traditions. The best time to visit is during the 'folk fiesta' on Wednesday and Friday afternoons, when folk dancers perform in the courtyard and women in traditional costume give displays of lacemaking and embroidery. There are free tastings of various foods, and the restaurant serves up hearty portions of typical Mallorcan fare. The tour of the house includes the family chapel, the medieval kitchens – and a dungeon with a torture chamber! ⓐ Carretera Esporles–Puigpunyent, Km 2, Esporles ⓣ 971 61 00 32 ⓦ www.lagranga.net Ⓛ Open 10.00– 19.00 (18.00 winter). Folk fiesta Wed and Fri 15.30–17.00. Equestrian Show Tues and Sun 13.15 and Thurs 16.00 ⓘ Admission fee

Lafiore Glass Factory ★★

Glass has been made on the island since Roman times and glass-making techniques have changed little since then. Here, you can watch craftsmen at work in the glass-blowing workshop, before visiting the shop next door where jugs, vases, drinking glasses and candleholders are the most popular buys. They also sell reproductions of antique Roman Glassware. ⓐ Carretera de Valldemossa, Km 11, S'Esgleieta ⓣ 971 61 01 40 ⓦ www.lafiore.com Ⓛ Open 08.00–20.00

Port de Valldemossa ★★

If you are brave enough to negotiate the 6km (3½ miles)-long helter-skelter drive that separates Valldemossa from its coastal port, you will enjoy numerous dramatic viewpoints and hair-raising hairpin bends before entering the charming fishing village of Port de Valldemossa. Here you will discover a handful of stone cottages, a few fishing boats and a small stony beach – perfect for a light lunch and a swim, before setting off again up the corkscrew road.

RESTAURANTS

Ca'n Pedro €€ A large, atmospheric cellar restaurant on the edge of the village, serving hearty Mallorcan fare and home-made desserts. Carrer Archiduque Luis Salvador, Valldemossa 971 61 21 70 Open 13.00–16.00 and 19.00–23.00; closed Sun night and Mon

Es Port € Set in Valldemossa's isolated fishing village, this small restaurant serves the freshest of fish and massive paellas. Port de Valldemossa 971 61 61 94 Restaurant open 11.30–17.30, bar 10.00–22.00

Meriendas € This cheap, cheerful locals' café serves sandwiches, cakes, pizzas and wickedly rich *xocolate* (hot chocolate). Vía Blanquerna, Valldemossa Open 08.00–20.00

Sa Cartoixa €€ Tumbet (Mallorcan ratatouille), rabbit stew, shoulder of lamb and paella are the specialities in this bustling café-restaurant, situated right at the heart of the village. Plaça Ramón Llull 5, Valldemossa 971 61 60 59 Open Sun–Fri 08.00–23.00

Vesubio € Traditional Italian restaurant with fresh pasta and home-made pizza dough. Star dish is saltimbocca – stuffed chicken breast. Extraordinary value. Archiduque Luis Salvador 23, Valldemossa 971 61 25 84 Open Thurs–Tues 13.00–16.00 and 20.00–23.00

Deià
the artists' village

The north-western coastline between Andratx and Deià contains some of the most spectacular scenery on Mallorca, with pine-scented forests and terraced hillsides tumbling into the sea. This corner of Mallorca has long appealed to foreigners – Frédéric Chopin and Robert Graves were both drawn here, and Michael Douglas and Richard Branson have homes in the area today.

Deià itself is a tiny village of ochre-coloured houses in the shadow of the Teix mountain. It was put on the map by the author and poet Robert Graves, who lived here from the 1930s until his death in 1985. He is buried beneath a simple hand-inscribed tombstone outside the church of Sant Joan Bautista at the top of the village. Deià has become a magnet for foreign artists over the last few decades and the village is full of small art galleries and chic cafés. Having explored, you may wish to take a drink or a meal at La Residencia, which used to belong to Richard Branson. Centrally located, this five-star hotel is set back off the main Deià road in beautiful gardens – but be warned, it is very pricey.

THINGS TO SEE & DO

Cala de Deià ★★

Just a 30-minute stroll from Deià, this tiny pebbly cove with its jagged cliffs and icy, clear waters is one of the hidden gems of Mallorca's north coast. There is even a ramshackle beach bar and a restaurant, Sa Caleta (see page 81), for refreshments.

Son Marroig ★★

Perched high above the north coast of the island with stunning sea views, this mansion was once the home of Mallorca's greatest admirer,

◀ *The romantic hillside village of Deià*

SHOPPING

Alic A tiny studio selling high-quality handmade ceramics and jewellery. Carrer Porxo 5, Deià Open 11.00–13.30 and 16.00–20.00 971 63 93 30 Closed most Sat afternoons and Sun

Arte This artisan's workshop sells unusual pottery, glass and olive-wood utensils. Plaça de la Iglesia 2, Deià 971 63 91 26 Open 10.00–13.00 and 15.00 and 19.00

the wealthy Austrian aristocrat and ecologist Archduke Luis Salvador. Known to the locals simply as S'Arxiduc, he spent the best part of his life here studying and recording Mallorcan wildlife and traditions. Today his house is open to the public, providing a fascinating insight into island life in the past. The garden houses a white-marble rotunda where he sat and contemplated the sea and Sa Foradada – a remarkable rocky headland jutting out to sea. Carretera Deià-Valldemossa Open Mon–Sat 09.30–14.00 and 15.00–19.30 (18.00 in winter) Admission charge

Deià Archaeological Museum ★

Small fascinating museum, worth visiting for the extremely attractive conversion of an old mill. Pre-historical finds from nearby caves. Es Clot 971 63 90 01 Open Tues, Thurs and Sun 17.00–19.00

RESTAURANTS & BARS

Bar Sa Fàbrica € For those who enjoy the cosy ambience of a small town bar, Jimmy will serve up a snack at any time. You can have a late drink and watch a match on TV. Carrer Arxiduc Luis Salvador 17 A 616 84 37 24 Open 16.00–03.30 (summer); noon–03.30 (winter)

Bens d'Avalls €€€ Very elegant and most suitable for a really special occasion with fabulous views of the rocky coastline with the sea beneath. Urb Costa Deià Ctra Sóller-Deià 971 63 23 81 Open Tues–Sun 13.00–15.00 and 20.15–01.00

Ca'n Costa €€ This restaurant serves traditional Mallorcan cooking (e.g. suckling pig) in a converted oil mill on the road from Valldemossa to Deià. Ⓐ Carretera Valldemossa–Deià Ⓣ 971 61 22 63 Ⓞ Open 12.30–16.00 and 19.30–midnight

Ca'n Quet €€€ Owned by the Es Moli Hotel, this restaurant is set away from the resort centre, heading south. The restaurant has a varied menu, which includes fish, meats and a good selection of wines and spirits. Ⓐ Carretera Valldemossa–Deià Ⓣ 971 63 91 96 Ⓞ Open 10.00–15.30 and 19.00–22.30; closed Mon

Jaime €€ Mallorcan dishes such as pork in cabbage leaves and baked fish, and a choice of seasonal specialties and home-made desserts. Ⓐ Carrer Arxiduc Luis Salvador 24 Ⓣ 971 63 90 29 Ⓞ Open Tues–Sun 13.00–17.00 and 19.30–23.00

Miradors de Na Foradada €€ This popular restaurant, clinging to a cliffside, specialises in Spanish and Mallorcan classics, such as paella. Ⓐ Carretera Valldemossa–Deià, Km 63 Ⓣ 971 63 90 26 Ⓞ Open Fri–Wed 12.30–15.30 and 19.30–20.00

La Pizzeria € Casual friendly atmosphere. Serves snails, paella and squid, as well as pizza and pasta dishes, plus a wide selection of wines. Ⓐ Carrer Archiduque Luis Salvador 13 Ⓣ 971 63 90 16 Ⓞ Open Thurs–Tues 13.00–16.00 and 20.00–22.30

Sa Caleta € Grilled squid, prawns and swordfish are the specialities in this seaview restaurant, perched high on the cliffs over a picturesque cove. Ⓐ Cala de Deià Ⓣ 971 63 91 37 Ⓞ Open 11.00–19.00

Sa Font Fresca € Family house turned into a classic, welcoming café offering a variety of *tapas* and sandwiches. A good place to join your friends for a drink and a game of table football. Ⓐ Carrer Arxiduc Luis Salvador 36 Ⓣ 971 63 94 41 Ⓞ Open Mon–Sat 07.00–22.30

Palma to Port de Sóller
the Mountain Express

The toytown train ride from Palma to Sóller is one of the highlights of any visit to Mallorca. The guards with their whistles, and the vintage carriages with their polished mahogany and brass panels, conjure up an image of a bygone age of travel. At the end of it all is a joyride down to the sea, in an antique tram imported from San Francisco.

The railway line, cut through the mountains in 1912, opened up Mallorca's previously inaccessible northern coastline to day-trippers from Palma. The tram service started the following year, and soon Port de Sóller became a fashionable resort. Nowadays the 'Mountain Express' is a must on every visitor's itinerary – with the result that the trains get very crowded at peak times. Five trains a day make the return journey from Palma, but unless you are a keen photographer, you can escape the worst of the crowds by avoiding the 10.40 *turístico* train. The only advantage of this train is that it makes an extra stop at a scenic viewpoint overlooking Sóller.

The best way to guarantee a seat on the train is to book an organised excursion through your holiday rep. Otherwise, at busy times, you may find that it is standing room only. More information is available at ⓦ www.sollernet.com/trendesoller.

THINGS TO SEE & DO

Boat trips ★★

Some of the finest views of Port de Sóller and the Serra de Tramuntana mountains beyond can only be seen from the sea. Hop on a pleasure cruise from the port to Sa Calobra to see the spectacular **Torrent de Pareis**, Mallorca's Grand Canyon, where a narrow gorge empties into the sea across a shingle beach. Don't forget to take your camera.

Bunyola ★★

The train rattles through the back streets of Palma and out on to the plain, passing almond and orange groves before climbing to the hill village of Bunyola. If you want to break your journey, you can get off here to explore this pretty village and to visit the Tunel factory, where many of Mallorca's herb-based liqueurs are made. Be sure to try the *palo*, a sweet carob-based liqueur. ⓐ Carrer Vinyetes, Bunyola

Take the antique tram down to the sea

Mirador del Pujol d'en Banya ★★

From Bunyola the train travels through a series of 13 tunnels – the longest one, Tunel Major, is just over 3 km (1½ miles) long. The 10.40 tourist train then stops at this *mirador* (panorama), with excellent views of the Sóller valley below. Even if you're not on this train, you can still enjoy a quick glimpse of the view as you pass. From here the train makes a curving descent towards Sóller, with the town appearing first to your left, and then to your right, as the track winds its way down the mountainside.

Port de Sóller ★★★

The Orange Express trams from Sóller to its port leave every 30 minutes from the station and the main square, passing through orchards of citrus fruit on their way down to the sea. Port de Sóller, with its wide sandy beach, makes an excellent place to stop for a couple of hours, wandering up to the lighthouse for scenic views of the port or enjoying a long lunch at one of the seafront restaurants. If you have time you can even take a boat cruise around the north coast from here.

Sóller ★★

The railway station at Sóller, based in a 17th-century manor house with overhanging jacaranda trees, is yet another throwback to the past. The town itself is well worth exploring (pages 86–89) for a couple of hours.

THE WAY BACK

From Port de Sóller there are several options for the return journey. The last train to Palma leaves Sóller at 19.00 (19.35 in high summer) and to catch it you must take the 18.00 tram from the port. An alternative, if you feel like a change of scenery, is the bus journey to Palma, passing through the villages of Deià (page 79) and Valldemossa (page 74). There is also a faster bus route through the Sóller tunnel, which opened in 1997. Just think – if the tunnel had been there before, the railway would never have been built!

BEACHES

The two beaches at **Port de Sóller** are the only sandy ones along the entire northern coast until **Cala Sant Vicenç** (see page 38). The main beach runs beside the tramway. The second beach – **Platja d'en Repic** – fronts an attractive pedestrian promenade and is usually quieter. Both beaches have sunbeds, sunshades and pedalos for hire, and there is also a windsurfing school.

RESTAURANTS

Es Faro €€ Enjoy delicious fish dishes at the 'The Lighthouse', served on a terrace high above the port affording exceptional coastal views. Leave room for a delicious home-made dessert. Carretera Faro, Cap Gros de Muleta 971 63 37 52 Open 12.30–15.30 and 20.00–23.00, Sun 19.00–22.00; closed Tues in winter

El Sólleric € International cooking on the beach, with a large terrace and private beach. You can even order from your sunbed by the sea! Platja d'en Repic, Port de Sóller 971 63 49 54 Open 07.30–late

Sa Llotja des Peix €€€ Upmarket fish restaurant overlooking the fishing harbour at Port de Sóller. You can still see fishermen mending their nets down below. Mallorcan specialities and fresh fish. Moll dels Pescadors 971 63 16 57 Open noon–16.00 and 20.00–23.00; closed Tues in winter

NIGHTLIFE

Altamar Discoteca The biggest and best disco in town, playing a variety of music to appeal to all ages. Carrer Es Traves Open nightly 21.00–06.00 (mid June–Sept), Fri and Sat nights only rest of year

Club Bassic This small, trendy nightclub attracts a young crowd, eager to let their hair down and party all night. Carrer de Jaume Torrens 19 Open Mon–Sat 23.00–05.00

Sóller
authentic mountain town

The friendly market town of Sóller (pronounced 'soy-air'), nestling in the lush Valley of Oranges at the heart of the Serra de Tramuntana mountains, never fails to captivate its many visitors. Its attractions include a cool climate with crisp mountain air, traditional lifestyle, and architectural interest as well as culinary delights and excellent shopping facilities.

THINGS TO SEE & DO

Alfàbia ★

The fountains don't seem to work these days, but these gardens are lovely, green, cool and shady. Ⓐ Carretera Palma-Sóller (at the entrance to the Sóller tunnel) Ⓛ Open Mon–Fri 09.30–18.30, Sat 09.30–13.00 (May–Oct); Mon–Fri 09.30–17.30, Sat 09.30–13.00 (Nov-Apr) ⓘ Admission charge

Ca'n Det ★★

Farm producing oranges and olives, extracting the oil in a press that dates from the 16th century. Buy some extra virgin oil at the end of your visit. Visits by appointment. Ⓐ Ozona 8 Ⓣ 971 63 03 03

Can Oliveret ★★

Rolls, cakes and pastries baked on the premises. Irresistible desserts. Ⓐ Plaça Espanya 14 Ⓣ 971 63 45 09

Sa Fàbrica de Gelats ★★

This small ice cream factory is well known for its creamy ices made from the valley's famous oranges and lemons. You'll be spolit for choice with 25 varieties to choose from. Ⓐ Avenida C. Colom 13, Soller Ⓣ 971 63 17 08 Ⓦ www.gelatsoller.com Ⓛ Open 10.00–14.00 and 17.00–20.00

Lluc ★★

The monastery at Lluc – pronounced 'yook'– has been Mallorca's leading centre of pilgrimage ever since it was founded in the 13th century. Like so many Catholic holy places, this is connected with a miraculous statue of the Virgin. The story goes that not long after the Catalan invasion, a local shepherd boy discovered a dark wooden statue of the Virgin in a cave, where it had been hidden during the Moorish occupation of Mallorca. Eventually a chapel was built to house the statue and now people come from all over Spain to pay homage to La Moreneta ('the little dark one').

As well as the church where the statue is kept, there are also pleasant grounds for strolling and a Way of the Rosary designed by the famous

Lluc Monastery

Catalan architect Antoni Gaudí. The complex also contains a museum as well as several restaurants and cafés. 971 87 15 25 www.lluc.net Museum open 10.00–17.30 Admission charge Basilica open 08.00–20.00 Admission free

Museu de Sóller ★

This delightful 18th-century manor house is crammed with relics of old Sóller. Casa de Cultura, Carrer de sa Mar 11 971 63 02 00 (Sóller Tourist Office) Open Mon 11.00–17.00, Tues–Fri 10.00–18.00, Sat 10.00–14.00

RESTAURANTS

Bar Es Firo € Bar-restaurant serving hearty country-style tapas. Try lamb with peppers and aubergines, fish in chilli or snails with wild mushrooms. Plaça Constitució 10B Open 08.00–22.00

Bar El Tren € This small bar near the railway station is one of the best places to try a glass of freshly squeezed orange or lemon juice – and better value than the crowded cafés on the main square! Plaça d'Espanya 5 Open 07.30–20.00

Sa Cova €€ This restaurant on Sóller's main square serves standard international cuisine as well as Mallorcan specialities, such as rabbit with garlic. Plaça Constitució 7 971 63 32 22 Open 13.00–16.00 and 19.30–23.00

El Guia €€ An old-fashioned restaurant which serves staple Mallorcan cuisine. The *menú del día* is always excellent value. Carrer Castanyer 3 971 63 02 27 Open 13.00–15.00 and 20.00–22.00

Es Planet € Soak up the sun and the atmosphere on the pavement terrace of this popular café in the main square. Plaça Constitució 3 Open Mon–Sat 07.00–21.00; closed Sun

SHOPPING

The covered market on **Carrer Cristòfol Colóm** sells fresh produce daily and there is an open-air market in **Plaça del Mercat** on Saturdays 08.00–13.00.

Ben Calçat Small shoe-manufacturer specialising in traditional Balearic footwear. Ⓐ Carrer de sa Lluna 74 Ⓣ 971 63 28 74 Ⓛ Open 09.00–13.00 and 16.00–20.00; closed Sat afternoons and Sun

Ca'n Oliver This fabric shop sells the distinctive Mallorca *roba de llengües* – durable cotton cloth with colourful stripy red, green or blue patterns, commonly used on the island for curtains, bedspreads, wall furnishings, tableware and upholstery. Ⓐ Carrer de sa Lluna 25 Ⓣ 971 63 82 05 Ⓛ Open 09.15–13.30 and 17.00–20.00; closed Sat afternoons and Sun

Eugenio A treasure trove of Mallorcan pearls, fans and olive-wood souvenirs. Ⓐ Carrer Jeroni Estades 11-A, Sóller Ⓣ 971 63 09 84 Ⓛ Open 09.00–13.00 and 16.00–20.00; closed Sat afternoons and Sun

Fet a Sóller Quality products all 'made in Sóller'. Everything from bottle of virgin olive oil, hot and spicy *sobrasada* sausages and orange marmalade to pottery, fashions and funky T-shirts for the kids. Ⓐ Carrer Ses Marjades 2 Ⓣ 971 63 38 42 Ⓛ Open Mon–Sat 09.00–15.00, 17.00–20.00; closed Sun

Pastelería Ses Delicies Be sure to taste their mouth-watering plum cake and *tartaleta manzana* (tarts made from local citrus fruits). Ⓐ Plaça Constitució 12 Ⓛ Open Mon–Sat 10.00–19.00; closed Sun

Ses Porxeres €€ Located inside a high-ceilinged barn beside the gardens of Alfàbia, this restaurant is renowned throughout the island for its game dishes. The wild boar and pheasant dishes are particularly recommended. Ⓐ Carretera Palma–Sóller (at the entrance to the Sóller tunnel) Ⓣ 971 61 37 62 Ⓛ Open 13.30–15.30 and 20.30–23.00; closed Sun evenings and Mon

Pollença
typical Mallorcan town

Located between two hills, Pollença is the perfect Mallorcan town – a maze of narrow streets converging on a busy main square, where the traditions of café life and the siesta live on as if tourism had never been invented.

Don't miss the popular Sunday morning market, when the main square, Plaça Major, is lined with fruit and vegetable stalls, and artists set up their stalls in the back streets behind the church. Buy a traditional Mallorcan basket and go shopping the Mallorcan way.

THINGS TO SEE & DO

El Calvari ★★

A flight of 365 steps lined with tall cypress trees leads from the town centre to a small chapel with great views.

Pont Romà (Roman Bridge) ★

This double-arched bridge across the dried-up riverbed of Torrent de Sant Jordi probably dates from the Roman occupation of the 1st century AD.

Puig de María (Mary's Mountain) ★

On the outskirts of Pollença, this hill is crowned by an old hermitage and defensive tower at its summit. Allow about an hour to walk to the top.

BEACHES

Regular buses leave from Pollença for the nearby beaches at **Port de Pollença** (page 40) and **Cala Sant Vicenç** (page38).

Pollença has a maze of narrow streets

Enjoy Pollença's traditional café life

RESTAURANTS & BARS

Bar Centro € A chance to meet the locals in a genuine and bustling tapas bar, set in the town's back streets. Carrer Temple 3 971 53 00 06 Open 08.00–23.00; closed Wed

Bar Nou € This popular locals' bar serves good value, no-nonsense food at excellent prices. Set menu at night too. Carrer Antoni Maura 13 971 53 00 05 Restaurant open 13.00–16.00 and 18.30–23.00; bar open 11.00–midnight; closed Tues

Ca'n Costa €€€ Grilled duck breast with cherries is just one of the specialities at this formal French-style restaurant. Carrer Costa i Llobera 11 971 53 00 42 Open 21.00–23.00; closed Sun

El Cantonet €€ The emphasis is on fresh fish and seafood at this small, intimate restaurant in the back streets of town. Ⓐ Carrer Montision 20 Ⓣ 971 53 04 29 Ⓛ Open 19.00–23.00; closed Tues

Clivia €€ The speciality at this formal restaurant is sea bass baked in salt. The locals consider this one of the best restaurants in town. Ⓐ Avinguda Pollentia Ⓣ 971 53 36 35 Ⓛ Open 13.00–15.00 and 19.00–22.30; closed Mon and Wed lunchtimes in winter

La Fonda €€ Back street restaurant with wood-beamed ceiling and a definite taste of old Mallorcan charm. Baked fish, lamb seasoned with garlic and herbs. Very good duck. Ⓐ Carrer Antoni Maura 32 Ⓣ 971 53 47 51 Ⓛ Open 13.00–15.30 and 19.00–23.00; closed Mon

Il Giardino €€ Stylish Italian on the main square featuring sea bass in lemon sauce and steak in balsamic vinegar. Ⓐ Plaça Major 11 Ⓣ 971 53 43 02 Ⓛ Open 12.30–15.00 and 19.00–23.00

La Tetera € Treat yourself to home-made carrot or banana cake and other tempting goodies at this pleasant café behind the church. Ⓐ Carrer Temple 7 Ⓣ 971 53 07 82 Ⓛ Open Mon–Fri 10.00–22.00, Sat and Sun 10.00–15.00

LIFESTYLE
Island life

Food & drink

Restaurants in Mallorca cater for a wide range of tastes – in the larger resorts you can get anything from an English breakfast to a Chinese take-away. Traditional Mallorcan cuisine, however, is typically Mediterranean, making full use of local products – especially pork, fish and vegetables – and heavily flavoured with garlic, tomato and herbs.

Popular Mallorcan dishes include *frito mallorquín*, a fry-up of liver, potatoes and tomatoes, and *sopes mallorquínes*, a thick vegetable soup that contains slices of left-over brown bread, as well as the delicious *tumbet*, a ratatouille of potatoes, peppers and aubergines. The Mallorcans are hearty meat-eaters – charcoal grills are a speciality, along with roast suckling pig and shoulder of lamb. *Sobrasada* sausages, made by mincing raw pork with hot red peppers, can be seen hanging in butcher's shops and tapas bars, along with whole cured hams (*jamon serrano*). As for fish, lobster, prawns and sardines are always excellent, and sea bass baked in rock salt is a Mallorcan speciality.

PAELLA

The classic Spanish dish is *paella*, a mound of steaming rice flavoured with saffron and topped with everything from mussels and prawns to pieces of chicken. The Mallorcan equivalent is *arròs brut* ('dirty rice'), which uses chicken and pork but no seafood. Paella is available everywhere on Mallorca, but be wary of anyone who says they can serve it immediately – it takes at least 20 minutes to cook it properly.

TAPAS

These Spanish nibbles are designed to whet the appetite before a meal, but order enough of them and they can make a meal in themselves. They are usually lined up in a display cabinet along the bar in metal trays, so it is easy to pick out what you want. Typical *tapas* range from plates of ham, cheese and olives to more exotic offerings like fried squid rings, garlic snails, stuffed peppers and meatballs in tomato sauce.

Paella is a classic Spanish dish

OTHER SNACKS

For a simple lunchtime snack try *pa amb oli*, an open sandwich which consists of thick brown bread rubbed with tomato and olive oil, and topped with ham or cheese. Another popular snack is *tortilla*, a potato omelette which is usually served cold with bread. Most bars serve *bocadillos* (filled rolls), and bakeries are a good place for stocking up on picnic provisions. Look out for *coca* (a kind of thin Mallorcan pizza), *empanadas* (small pasties filled with meat, fish or spinach) and *ensaimadas* (spiral-shaped pastries that can be either savoury or sweet).

WINE & BEER

The *vino de la casa* (house wine) in most restaurants will probably be from Mallorca and is certainly worth a try. For something a bit more special, order a bottle of Rioja – these full-bodied, oak-aged wines come in both red and white varieties and are considered the best in Spain. Cava, or Spanish champagne, makes an inexpensive treat and is sometimes combined with fruit juices for a refreshing cocktail. Beer (*cerveza*) is usually lager, sold either bottled or on draught – if you want draught, ask for *una caña*. Bars in the resorts have a wide selection of imported beers from Britain, Germany and elsewhere.

OTHER ALCOHOLIC DRINKS

Sherry (*fino*), served bone-dry and chilled, is the perfect drink to accompany a plate of ham before a meal. Another refreshing drink is *sangría*, an alcoholic fruit punch based on red wine, brandy and lemonade – delicious, but much more potent than it tastes. Most bars stock a good selection of Spanish brandies – popular brands include Soberano and Fundador – but for a truly local drink try *hierbas*, a herb-based Mallorcan liqueur which comes either sweet or dry.

TIPPING

Restaurant bills include a service charge but it is usual to leave an extra tip of around 5–10 per cent for good service. In bars, the custom is to leave your small change behind.

SOFT DRINKS

The tap water is not always safe to drink in Mallorca, so most people prefer to drink mineral water – *agua con gas* is sparkling, *agua sin gas* is still. Popular drinks, such as Coca-Cola and lemonade, are available everywhere, and some bars offer freshly squeezed orange and lemon juice or *granizado*, which is a fruit drink with crushed ice. The Spanish always drink *café solo* after a meal – which is a small shot of strong, dark coffee, like an espresso – but visitors should have no trouble ordering other types of coffee such as *café con leche*, made with hot milk, or *descafeinado*, decaffeinated coffee. Tea *(té)* is also widely available in the resorts.

EATING OUT – A FEW TIPS

- The Spanish tend to eat very late. In most of the resorts it should be possible to get a meal at any time of day, but few restaurants in Palma open before 13.00 for lunch and 20.00 for dinner – and most people come a lot later than this.
- Many restaurants offer a *menú del día* at lunchtime – a set, three-course meal, often including wine or water, at a very good price. There is not always much choice but the food is always filling, local and fresh.
- Don't be afraid to try the local restaurants – almost all have English menus and even if they don't, the waiter will usually be able to explain what's on the menu.

Most bars stock a wide selection of local and imported drinks

Menu decoder

aceitunas aliñadas Marinated olives
albóndigas en salsa Meatballs in (usually tomato) sauce
albóndigas de pescado Fish cakes
allioli Garlic-flavoured mayonnaise served as an accompaniment to just about anything – a rice dish, vegetables, shellfish – or as a dip for bread
bistek or biftek Beef steak; rare is *poco hecho*, *regular* is medium and *muy hecho* is well done
bocadillo Sandwich, usually made of French-style bread
caldereta Stew based on fish or lamb
caldo Soup or broth
carne Meat; *carne de cerdo* is pork; *carne de cordero* is lamb; *carne picada* is minced meat; *carne de ternera* is beef;
chorizo Cured, dry red-coloured sausage made from chopped pork, paprika, spices, herbs and garlic
churros Flour fritters cooked in spiral shapes in very hot fat and cut into strips, best dunked into hot chocolate
cordero asado Roast lamb flavoured with lemon and white wine
embutidos charcuteria Pork meat preparations including *jamón* (ham), *chorizo* (see above), *salchichones* (sausages) and *morcillas* (black pudding)
ensalada Salad – usually composed of lettuce, onion, tomato and olives
ensalada mixta As above, but with extra ingredients, such as boiled egg, tuna fish or asparagus
escabeche Sauce of fish, meat or vegetables cooked in wine and vinegar and left to go cold
estofado de buey Beef stew, made with carrots and turnips, or with potatoes
fiambre Any type of cold meat such as ham, *chorizo*, etc
flan Caramel custard, the national dessert of Spain
fritura A fry-up, as in *fritura de pescado* – different kinds of fried fish
gambas Prawns; *gambas a la plancha* are grilled, *gambas al ajillo* are fried with garlic and *gambas con gabardina* deep fried in batter
gazpacho andaluz Cold soup (originally from Andalucia) made from tomatoes, cucumbers, peppers, bread, garlic and olive oil

gazpacho manchego Hot dish made with meat (chicken or rabbit) and unleavened bread (not to be confused with *gazpacho andaluz*)
habas con jamón Broad beans fried with diced ham (sometimes with chopped hard boiled egg and parsley)
helado Ice cream
jamón Ham; *jamón serrano* and *jamón iberico* (far more expensive) are dry cured; cooked ham is *jamón de york*
langostinos a la plancha Large prawns grilled and served with vinaigrette or *allioli*; *langostinos a la marinera* are cooked in white wine
lenguado Sole, often served cooked with wine and mushrooms
mariscos Shellfish
menestra A dish of mixed vegetables cooked separately and combined before serving
menú del día Set menu for the day at a fixed price; it may or may not include bread, wine and a dessert, but it doesn't usually include coffee
paella Famous rice dish originally from Valencia but now made all over Spain; *paella valenciana* has chicken and rabbit; *paella de mariscos* is made with seafood; *paella mixta* combines meat and seafood
pan Bread; pan de molde is sliced white bread; wholemeal bread is *pan integral*
pincho moruno Pork kebab: spicy chunks of pork on a skewer
pisto Spanish version of ratatouille, made with tomato, peppers, onions, garlic, courgette and aubergines
pollo al ajillo Chicken fried with garlic; *pollo a la cerveza* is cooked in beer; *pollo al chilindrón* is cooked with peppers, tomatoes and onions
salpicón de mariscos Seafood salad
sopa de ajo Delicious warming winter garlic soup thickened with bread, usually with a poached egg floating in it
tarta helada Popular ice-cream cake served as dessert
ternasco asado Roast lamb flavoured with lemon and white wine
tortilla de patatas Classic omelette, also called *tortilla española*, made with potatoes that can be eaten hot or cold
zarzuela de pescado y mariscos Stew made with white fish and shellfish in a tomato, wine and saffron stock

Mallorcan pottery

Shopping

GLASSWARE

You can watch glass being made at the **Lafiore factory**, just outside Palma on the road to Valldemossa, or at **Ca'n Gordiola**, a glass-blowing workshop housed in a mock castle between Palma and Manacor. Many of the ornaments here come in striking blue and green designs.

LEATHER & SUEDE

Inca, in island's centre, is Mallorca's third-largest town and is known as the 'leather town' because of the number of factories producing leather goods. Factory showrooms sell a wide range, from boots and shoes to handbags, jackets and belts. The quality varies and it pays to shop around – you will usually be offered a small discount if you buy in the factory shop, but you may find that prices are just as keen at a market or in the resorts. On Thursday mornings Inca is the setting for Mallorca's biggest traditional market, selling everything from fresh fruit to fine leather bags.

PEARLS

Majorica pearls come from a factory in Manacor – a few kilometres inland from Porto Cristo. You can visit some of the factories to watch the pearls being made and make purchases in their shops.

POTTERY

Rustic earthenware cooking pots make a good buy at country markets, together with *plats morenos*, glazed bowls painted with symbols of cockerels or flowers. A popular souvenir, especially for children, is a *siurell* – a clay whistle, painted white with splashes of red and green.

WOODCARVING

Sturdy bowls of carved olive wood make an excellent present – you can also find olive-wood ashtrays, coasters, eggcups and even ear-rings. **OlivArt**, a large factory shop at the entrance to Manacor from Palma, has the biggest selection of olive-wood souvenirs on the island.

Kids

ANIMALS & ZOOS

Children always enjoy encounters with animals, and on the drive through the **Safari-Zoo** near Sa Coma (page 53), they will get the chance to see zebra, giraffes, elephants and ostriches at close quarters. Take a tour of the zoo on the mini-train and they will enjoy it twice as much. Dolphins, sea lions and parrots perform acrobatics at **Marineland**, near Palma Nova (page 22), where there are also sharks, monkeys and tropical birds on display. There are more parrots at **Jumaica** near Cales de Mallorca (page 61) and more tropical fish at **Mallorca Aquarium** at Porto Cristo (page 58).

MINI-GOLF

There are mini-golf courses in most of the resorts, but four of them have been developed into massive 54-hole complexes with enough other activities and attractions to occupy most of the day. These are **Golf Fantasia** at Palmanova (page 22) and at S'Arenal (page 70), **Golf Paradis** at Sa Coma (page 56) and **Super Golf**, part of the Hidropark water park at Alcúdia (page 45).

WATER PARKS

In hot weather, children like nothing more than splashing about in the water and if they tire of the beach you can always take them to one of Mallorca's water parks, where there will be enough pools, chutes and slides to keep them happy for hours. The biggest of all, with some thrilling rides, is **Aqualand** at S'Arenal (page 70), and others are to be found at **Aqualand** in Magaluf (page 24) and **Hidropark** in Port d'Alcúdia (page 45). There is also a small water park attached to the wax museum at El Foro de Mallorca near Binissalem, on the Mallorcan Plains. Some of these can be visited on organised excursions, booked through your holiday representative, as well as independently.

Sea lions at Marineland near Palma Nova

Sports & activities

ON THE GREENS

Many people come to Mallorca for the excellent golf facilities, with 18 excellent courses offering a variety of different challenges as well as some magnificent sea views. Most are situated close to the resorts. Clubs, trolleys and buggies are available for hire at each of the courses. Shorts are allowed, but golfers are asked not to come in their beach gear.

Andratx Golf Club ⓐ Carrer M. Cena 39, Camp de Mar ⓣ 971 23 62 80
Canyamel Golf Club ⓐ Near Cala Rajada ⓣ 971 84 13 13
Capdepera Golf Club ⓐ Roca Viva, near Cala Rajada ⓣ 971 81 85 00
Club de Golf de Pula ⓐ Near Cala Rajada ⓣ 971 81 70 34
Club de Golf Son Servera ⓐ Near Cala Millor ⓣ 971 84 00 96
ⓘ Nine holes
Golf Pollença ⓐ Near Pollença ⓣ 971 53 32 16 ⓘ Nine holes
Golf Poniente ⓐ Near Magaluf ⓣ 971 13 01 48
Golf Santa Ponça 1 ⓐ Near Santa Ponça ⓣ 971 69 02 11
Golf Vall d'Or ⓐ Near Cala d'Or ⓣ 971 83 70 68
Real Golf de Bendinat ⓐ Near Illetes ⓣ 971 40 52 00
Son Antem Golf Resort and Spa ⓐ Marriott Mallorca ⓣ 971 12 92 00
ⓘ Two 18 hole courses
Son Termens Golf Club ⓐ Ctra de S'Esgleita, Km 10 Bunyola
ⓣ 971 61 78 62
Son Vida Golf ⓐ Near Palma ⓣ 971 79 12 10

WALKING & CYCLING

Mallorca offers plenty of opportunities for keen walkers and cyclists, from serious mountain challenges to flat coastal paths. The best hiking is to be found in the Serra de Tramuntana mountains along the north coast, but there are also plenty of good walks close to the resorts. Bicycles can be hired in most of the resorts and are a good way to explore the gentle countryside of the Mallorcan Plains. An easy, flat

Windsurfing is very popular on Mallorca

cycle path runs alongside the coast road between Alcúdia and Ca'n Picafort on Alcúdia Bay, enabling you to reach the S'Albufera nature reserve or to stop off at a lonely, dune-backed beach which cannot be reached by car.

IN THE WATER

Once you have got used to swimming in the sea, it does not take much extra effort to add a bit of snorkelling to the experience. Flippers and masks can be bought in a number of resort shops, allowing you to swim out into the crystal-clear water and peer down at the marine life beneath the surface. For a true underwater experience, you can learn to scuba dive. Most resorts have diving schools with trained professional instructors, where you can learn the ropes, go on diving excursions and get close to some of the colourful underwater life that most people only see from glass-bottomed boats. These include **Centro de Buceo Zoea** at Santa Ponça (t 971 69 14 44 w www.zoea.com), **Scuba Pollentia** at Port de Pollença (t 971 86 79 78) and **Michael's Diving School** at Cala d'Or (t 971 82 40 35). Remember that diving is only for experienced swimmers and that you should complete your last dive at least 24 hours before your flight home.

ON THE WATER

The calm waters around the Mallorcan coast provide ideal conditions for windsurfing and for sailing in dinghies and catamarans. Sailboards are available for hire at most of the major beaches, and sometimes tuition is available as well. Sailing boats can be hired from **Sail and Surf Pollença** at Port de Pollença (t 971 86 53 46) as well as at Cala d'Or and Font de Sa Cala near Cala Rajada. Beginners will obviously need to stay close to the coast, but more experienced sailors can head off in search of remote beaches and deserted coves. For more high-octane thrills, sports such as waterskiing are available at some of the larger resorts – while if all you want is a gentle ride and a bit of exercise, you can hire out a pedalo or a canoe.

Festivals & events

CONCERTS

Classical music lovers should head for Pollença during the summer – the International Music Festival, held in the courtyard of a Dominican monastery between July and September each year, attracts leading musicians from all over Europe.

FESTIVALS

Mallorca's traditional festivals are one of the best places to meet the local people and experience the atmosphere of Mallorcan life. Every town and village celebrates its own saint's day, with street parties, music, dancing, fireworks, fancy-dress parades and general merriment. Many of the festivals are religious in origin, while others recall significant moments in Mallorcan history. Here is a summer guide to some of the most important events:

May

Moors and Christians Sóller is 'defended' against an 'invasion' of Moors in a stirring recreation of Mallorcan history – usually 8 and 10 May.

June

Saint Peter The patron saint of fishermen is honoured with processions of fishing boats in the island's ports on 28 and 29 June.

July

Fishermen's Festival Another procession of fishing boats, this time in honour of the Virgin Mary, is held across Mallorca on 16 July. Porto Cristo has one of the best events.

August

Moors and Christians More 'battles' between historic enemies, this time in Pollença on the 2nd August.

Cavallets The famous annual festival of Felanitx, in which children dressed as hobby horses are chased through the streets by giants, takes place on 28 August.

September

Tourist Week Cala Rajada lays on a week of festivities for visitors, including folk dancing, Spanish music and firework displays.

FLAMENCO & FOLK DANCE

Flamenco is a gypsy folk dance which originated in southern Spain but is now performed all over the country, and you can experience flamenco and Mallorcan folk dancing in the evening at some resort hotels. For a really memorable evening, head for Son Amar, Mallorca's top nightspot, where the all-star cabaret show (with dinner) features flamenco and Spanish dancing from the Carmen Mota ballet, who performed at the opening ceremony for the 1992 Barcelona Olympics. Tickets for this are usually booked up in advance, so it is best to arrange it through your resort representative. **Casino Mallorca** near Magaluf (☎ 971 13 00 00) also has dinner shows with performances of flamenco and folk dancing on occasions.

To find out what is happening in your area, ask at the local Tourist Office or pick up a free copy of *Where to go*, a newsletter published in English every three months. Concerts, plays and other events are also listed each day in the *Majorca Daily Bulletin*.

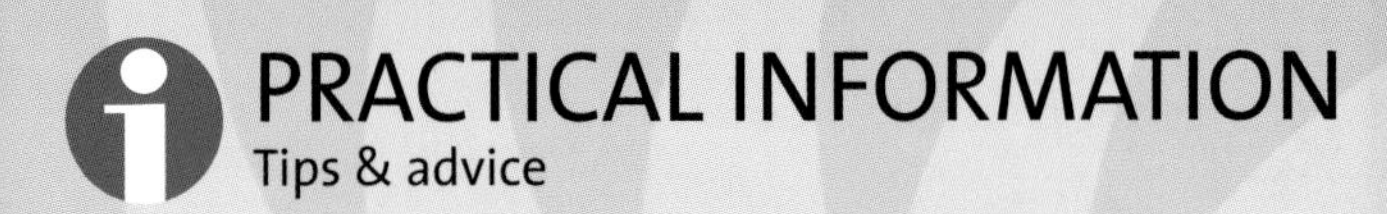

PRACTICAL INFORMATION

Tips & advice

Preparing to go

GETTING THERE

The cheapest way to get to Mallorca is to book a package holiday with one of the leading tour operators specialising in Spanish holidays. You should also check the Travel supplements of weekend newspapers, such as the *Sunday Telegraph*, and the *Sunday Times*. They often carry adverts for inexpensive flights, as well as classified adverts for privately owned villas and apartments to rent in most popular holiday destinations.

If your travelling times are flexible, and if you can avoid the school holidays, you can also find some very cheap last-minute deals using the websites for the leading holiday companies.

BY AIR

Mallorca is well-served by charter flights and, for independent travellers, there are several no-frills airlines operating from airports around the UK. Information and on-line reservations can be made though the websites of leading tour operators.

BY SEA

Regular car ferries operate from Barcelona and Valencia on the Spanish mainland. Reservations can be made in advance and on arrival at the port. Crossings normally take 8 hours but there are also fast catamarans that do the run in 3 hours 15 minutes.

TOURIST INFORMATION

The Palma de Mallorca council has a useful website (Ⓦ www.a-palma.es) as does the Ministry of Tourism (Ⓦ www.visitbalears.com). Unfortunately, not all the pages are translated and some of the English is a little difficult to follow. However, if you enter Mallorca (or the alternative spelling of Mallorca) in any search engine, you will find a wealth of pages on every aspect, hotels, resorts, water sports, golf, etc., in English.

BEFORE YOU LEAVE

Holidays should be about fun and relaxation, so avoid last minute panics and stress by making your preparations well in advance.

It is not necessary to have inoculations to travel in Europe, but you should make sure you and your family are up to date with the basics, such as tetanus. It is a good idea to pack a small first-aid kit to carry with you containing plasters, antiseptic cream, travel sickness pills, insect repellent and/or bite relief cream, antihistamine tablets, upset stomach remedies and painkillers. Sun lotion can be more expensive in Mallorca than in the UK so it is worth taking a good selection especially of the higher factor lotions if you are taking children with you, and don't forget after-sun cream as well. If you are taking prescription medicines, ensure that you take enough for the duration of your visit – you may find it impossible to obtain the same medicines in Mallorca. It is also worth having a dental check-up before you go.

DOCUMENTS

The most important documents you will need are your tickets and your passport. Check well in advance that your passport is up to date and has at least three months left to run (six months is even better). All children, including newborn babies, need their own passport now, unless they are already included on the passport of the person they are travelling with. It generally takes at least three weeks to process a passport renewal. This can be longer in the run-up to the summer months. For the latest information on how to renew your passport and the processing times call the **Passport Agency** on ⓣ 0870 521 0410, or access their website ⓦ www.ukpa.gov.uk

You should check the details of your travel tickets well before your departure, ensuring that the timings and dates are correct.

If you are thinking of hiring a car while you are away, you will need to have your UK driving licence with you. If you want more than one driver for the car, the other drivers must have their licence too.

MONEY

You will need some currency before you go, especially if your flight gets you to your destination at the weekend or late in the day after the banks have closed. Traveller's cheques are the safest way to carry money because the money will be refunded if the cheques are lost or stolen. To buy traveller's cheques or exchange money at a bank you may need to give up to a week's notice, depending on the quantity of foreign currency you require. You can exchange money at the airport before you depart. You should also make sure that your credit, charge and debit cards are up to date – you do not want them to expire mid holiday – and that your credit limit is sufficient to allow you to make those holiday purchases. Don't forget, too, to check your PIN numbers in case you haven't used them for a while – you may want to draw money from cash dispensers while you are away. You will also need your PIN number for every credit card transaction.

INSURANCE

Have you got sufficient cover for your holiday? Check that your policy covers you adequately for loss of possessions and valuables, for activities you might want to try – such as scuba-diving, horse-riding, or water sports – and for emergency medical and dental treatment, including flights home if required.

After January 2006, a new EHIC card replaces the E111 form to allow UK visitors access to reduced-cost, and sometimes free state-provided medical treatment in the EEA. For further information, ring EHIC enquiries line: ⓣ 0845 605 0707, or visit the Department of Health website ⓦ www.dh.gov.uk

CLIMATE

Mallorca is warm and sunny between April and September and at its hottest in June, July and August when light clothing is all that's necessary. Otherwise, a jacket is a good idea for the evening. Rain is normal

between October and February and it can be quite chilly. Strong sunblock cream is advisable even when cloudy. Be extra careful with children and keep them out of the midday sun.

PETS

Remember to make arrangements for the care of your pets while you are away – book them into a reputable cat or dog hotel, or make arrangements with a trustworthy neighbour to ensure that they are properly fed, watered and exercised while you are on holiday.

SECURITY

Take sensible precautions to prevent your house being burgled while you are away:

- Cancel milk, newspapers and other regular deliveries so that post and milk does not pile up on the doorstep, indicating that you are away.
- Let the postman know where to leave parcels and bulky mail that will not go through your letterbox – ideally with a next-door neighbour.
- If possible, arrange for a friend or neighbour to visit regularly, closing and opening curtains in the evening and morning, and switching lights on and off to give the impression that the house is being lived in.
- Consider buying electrical timing devices that will switch lights and radios on and off, again to give the impression that there is someone in the house.
- Let Neighbourhood Watch representatives know that you will be away so that they can keep an eye on your home.
- If you have a burglar alarm, make sure that it is serviced and working properly and is switched on when you leave (you may find that your insurance policy requires this). Ensure that a neighbour is able to gain access to the alarm to turn it off if it is set off accidentally.
- If you are leaving cars unattended, put them in a garage, if possible, and leave a key with a neighbour in case the alarm goes off.

AIRPORT PARKING & ACCOMMODATION

If you intend to leave your car in an airport car park while you are away, or stay the night at an airport hotel before or after your flight, you should book ahead to take advantage of discounts or cheap off-airport parking. Airport accommodation gets booked up several weeks in advance, especially during the height of the season. Check whether the hotel offers free parking for the duration of the holiday – often the savings made on parking costs can reduce the accommodation price.

PACKING TIPS

Baggage allowances vary according to the airline, destination and the class of travel, but 20kg (44lb) per person is the norm for luggage that is carried in the hold (it usually tells you what the weight limit is on your ticket). You are also allowed one item of cabin baggage weighing no more than 5 kg, (11lb) and measuring 46 x 30 x 23cm (18 x 12 x 9 inches). In addition, you can usually carry your duty-free purchases, umbrella, handbag, coat, camera, etc, as hand baggage. Large items – surfboards, golf-clubs, collapsible wheelchairs and pushchairs – are usually charged as extras and it is a good idea to let the airline know in advance that you want to bring these.

CHECK-IN, PASSPORT CONTROL AND CUSTOMS

First-time travellers can often find airport security intimidating, but it is all very easy really.

- Check-in desks usually open two or three hours before the flight is due to depart. Arrive early for the best choice of seats.
- Look for your flight number on the TV monitors in the check-in area, and find the relevant check-in desk. Your tickets will be checked and your luggage taken. Take your boarding card and go to the departure gate. Here hand luggage will be X-rayed and your passport checked.
- In the departure area, you can shop and relax, but watch the monitors that tell you when to board – usually about 30 minutes before take-off. Go to the departure gate shown on the monitor and follow the instructions given to you by the airline staff.

During your stay

AIRPORTS

Arrivals Son Sant Juan Airport, Palma, is an international airport with all facilities. Wheelchairs are available on request and there are moving walkways to shorten the distances involved. There are car rental, hotel reservations, currency exchange and tourist information offices in the main arrivals hall. The taxi stand is just outside and there is an express bus (no. 1) to and from Palma.

Departures There are several shops and a large duty free shop although you will find prices are cheaper in your nearest hypermarket or even the local supermarket.

There may be delays during peak periods so charter flight passengers should keep some currency handy. If delays are lengthy, there are normally clowns and other entertainment to amuse the children.

On flight information screens *retrasado* means delayed and *embarcando* embarking.

Arrival and departure information Ⓦ www.aena.es

Airport Information desk Ⓣ 971 78 90 99

BEACHES

Swimming in Mallorca is generally safe but look out for the red warning flags on the larger beaches and never go in when they are flying. Other beaches may be safe for swimming but there are unlikely to be life-saving amenities available. Bear in mind that the weather can change rapidly at the beginning and end of the holiday season and strong currents can develop, turning a safe beach into a not-so-safe one. If in doubt, ask your local representative or at your hotel.

TELEPHONING MALLORCA

To call Mallorca from the UK, dial 00 34 then the nine-digit number – there's no need to wait for a dialling tone.

BEACH ETIQUETTE

Topless bathing is acceptable on most Mallorcan beaches, though nudity is only permitted at **Es Trenc** on the south coast and **Platja Mago** near Magaluf. While attitudes have relaxed about wearing beachware off the beach, tourists should dress more appropriately while walking in resorts and towns especially Palma itself.

CHILDREN'S ACTIVITIES

Many hotels organise games and sports during the day supervised by trained monitors. There are evening discos and other entertainment according to age groups. Water sports of all kinds, for beginners and the more advanced, can be found on the nearest beach and there are water theme parks for thrilling rides, dolphin shows, mini-golf, even go-karting in Magaluf (see page 102).

CONSULATE

British Consulate The Consulate is there to give advice and replace lost passports but staff will not become involved in any holiday/hotel problems which are the province of the hotel/tour operator. They can give advice on transferring money and provide a list of lawyers, English-speaking doctors, dentists, etc. ⓐ Plaça Major 3D, Palma ⓣ 971 71 24 45 ◔ Open Mon–Fri 08.00–15.30

CURRENCY

As an EU Member State, the currency in Spain is now the euro (€). Exchange rates are shown in all banks and currency exchange bureaux. There is a €1 and a €2 coin in addition to 50, 20, 10, 5, 2 and 1 *centímo* coins. There are 500, 200, 100, 50, 20, 10 and 5 € banknotes. Each country mints its own coins with a different 'heads' side but a common 'tails'. Therefore you could easily find yourself making your purchase with French or Italian coins and receiving change in Greek or German coins but all are equally acceptable in Spain!

ELECTRICITY

Electricity is supplied at 220–225 volts. Spanish plugs are of the two-pin round plug variety so an adapter will be required for British and non-Continental appliances. If you are considering buying electrical appliances to take home, always check that they will work in the UK before you buy.

FACILITIES FOR THE DISABLED

Although the authorities are aware of the problems hampering ease of movement by disabled visitors and great strides are being made in smoothing their way, replacing steps by ramps for example, much still remains to be done. Check with your travel company on the hotels that provide facilities for the disabled.

The Calvià Council provides sea bathing chairs free of charge on its beaches at Palma Nova, Magaluf, Santa Ponça, Peguera (Torà beach) and Ses Illetes (971 13 91 39). For information on activities contact **Aspayn** 971 77 03 09 or **Asprom** 971 28 90 52
Taxis www.cruzroja.es

GETTING AROUND

Car hire and driving There is plenty of choice of car hire companies. Drivers should be over 21 and have held a driving licence for one year. Fully comprehensive insurance is advisable. Seat belts are compulsory in the front seats and, where fitted, in the back seats. Children under 12 must sit in the back. Drive on the right.

The speed limits in force are 120km/h (75mph) on motorways, 100km/h (63mph) on dual carriageways and 90km/h (55mph) on single carriageways except in urban areas where it is 50km/h (32mph). The Guardia Civil, the police in green uniforms, patrol the highways, issue fines and carry out breathalyser tests. These are very strict, with limits of 0.5g per litre and 0.3g per litre for drivers who have held a licence for less than two years.

If you meet a coach on a narrow twisting mountain road, going up or down, you are the one who must reverse. There are few public phones on motorways if you do have a breakdown. There is an extensive network of petrol stations on the island. Some are self-service, many stay open 24 hours and all accept credit cards. Note, however, that no change is given between 21.00 and 08.00.

There are several underground car parks in Palma and several more in the pipeline. The one by the cathedral and under the Plaçá Major are undoubtedly the most popular so be prepared to queue. Palma and many other towns operate restricted parking areas, known as ORA. Tickets can be obtained from nearby machines and should be displayed inside the windscreen. There is a discount on parking and speeding fines that are paid promptly at the nearest town hall or the bank listed on the ticket.

Buses The bus service is good but buses do get very crowded in summer. Routes are available from the tourist information office. The driver is paid on entering, so try and have small change ready.

Trains A narrow-gauge railway runs from Palma to Inca (the leather town), on to Sa Pobla (which provides the first new potatoes in the UK, in time for Christmas dinner) and then on to Manacor. The journey lasts for about 50 minutes. An old wooden train runs from Palma to Sóller on the northern coast, a journey of some 55 mins. The Port de Sóller is a short ride away by an equally old wooden tram.

Taxis These are now mainly white. It's very common for a taxi taking new arrivals from the airport to their hotel to cost three times as much as it will cost them from their hotel to the airport on departure. Enquire about the fare before setting off but if you feel you have been over-charged, ask for a receipt so that you can make an official complaint at the Dirección General de Consumo (equivalent of the UK Consumers Ombudsman) ⓐ Carrer Sant Gaietà 3, Palma ⓣ 971 17 62 62

Beach trains Several resorts have beach trains that run alongside the sea and are a delightful way of travelling to your favourite spot on the beach.

Horse drawn carriages *Galeras* are an alternative choice for sightseeing in Palma. There are ranks beside the Cathedral and the Passeig de Sagrera, with a list of fares.

In hot climates, it is important to use a strong sunblock

HEALTH MATTERS

Health hazards People who are not used to the sun burn easily and children are especially vulnerable. It is a good idea to cover up with a strong sunblock, to wear a hat and to keep out of the midday sun by taking a siesta in the shade. In a hot climate you also need to drink a lot more water and soft drinks. Although the water is probably quite safe to drink, it can be very salty around the coast or heavily chlorinated. Bottled water is advisable, either still water *(agua sin gas)* or fizzy water *(agua con gas)*.

A change of diet could lead to tummy upsets so carry a supply of anti-diarrhoea tablets. Prevent dehydration by drinking plenty of liquids and relax in the shade during the hottest part of the day. However, if you do run into problems, there is an extensive network of health centres *(centres de salut)* and helpful chemists *(farmacias*, identified by a green cross) to advise you. A list of chemists open out of hours is shown in their windows and published in the *Majorca Daily Bulletin*. A second ultra-modern public hospital opened on the outskirts of Palma in 2000. As in so many countries, AIDs is present in Spain. Condoms are available.

Mosquitoes can be a problem at the beginning and end of summer. It's best to cover up in the evenings, use an insect repellent on any exposed skin, and use a plug-in device in your room to keep the mosquitoes at bay.

THE LANGUAGE

Nobody expects tourists to be good at Mallorquín, but it is always nice to be able to say a few words in the national language. Spanish will get you by everywhere – and most people working in the resorts, especially waiters, barmen and taxi-drivers, speak excellent English and German.

ENGLISH	**SPANISH (pronunciation)**
General vocabulary	
yes	*sí (see)*
no	*no (no)*
please	*por favor (por faBOR)*
thank you (very much)	*(muchas) gracias (MOOchas GRAtheeyas)*
You're welcome	*de nada (deNAda)*
hello	*hola (Ola)*
goodbye	*adiós (adeeYOS)*
good morning/day	*buenos días (BWEnos DEEyas)*
good afternoon/evening	*buenas tardes (BWEnas TARdes)*
good evening (after dark)/night	*buenas noches (BWEnas NOches)*
excuse me (to get attention or to get past)	*¡disculpe! (desKOOLpay)*
excuse me (to apologise or to ask pardon)	*¡perdón! (perDON)*
Sorry	*lo siento (lo seeYENtoe)*
Help!	*¡socorro! (SOHcohroe)*
today	*hoy (oy)*
tomorrow	*mañana (manYAna)*
yesterday	*ayer (ayYER)*
Useful words and phrases	
open	*abierto (abeeYERtoe)*
closed	*cerrado (therRAdoe)*
push	*empujar (empooYAR)*
pull	*tirar (teeRAR)*

ENGLISH	**SPANISH (pronunciation)**
Useful words and phrases	
How much is it?	*¿Cuánto es? (KWANtoe es)*
expensive	*caro/a (KARo/a)*
bank	*el banco (el BANko)*
bureau de change	*la oficina de cambio (la ofeeTHEEna de KAMbeeyo)*
post office	*correos (koRAYos)*
duty (all-night) chemist	*la farmacia de guardia (la farMAHtheeya de garDEEya)*
bank card	*la tarjeta de banco (la tarHEHta de BANko)*
credit card	*la tarjeta de crédito (la tarHEHta de CREdeetoe)*
traveller's cheques	*los cheques de viaje (los CHEkes de beeAhay)*
table	*la mesa (la MEHsa)*
menu	*el menú/la carta (el menOO/la KARta)*
waiter	*el/la camarero/a (el/la kahmahRERo/a)*
water	*agua (Agwa)*
fizzy/still water	*agua con/sin gas (Agwa con/sin gas)*
I don't understand	*no entiendo (No enteeYENdoe)*
The bill, please	*La cuenta, por favor (la KWENta, por faBOR)*
Do you speak English?	*¿Habla usted inglés? (Ablah OOsted eenGLES)*
My name is...	*Me llamo ... (meh YAmoh ...)*
Where are the toilets?	*¿Dónde están los servicios? (DONdeh esTAN los serBEEtheeos)*
Where is there a telephone?	*¿Dónde está un teléfono? (DONdeh esTAH oon teLEfono)*
Can you call me a taxi?	*¿Puede llamar a un taxi? (PWEday yaMAR ah oon TAKsee)*
Can you help me?	*¿Puede ayudarme?*

EMERGENCY TELEPHONE NUMBER
For police, fire or ambulance the number is **112** (English spoken).

MEDIA

British daily newspapers are widely available and the *Majorca Daily Bulletin* provides wide coverage of local events and English sport. There is also the *Reader*, a weekly newspaper, and a free quarterly publication *Where to go* published by the tourist information office. Satellite television is everywhere, so you won't miss any important matches!

OPENING HOURS

The *siesta* is still a time-honoured custom in Mallorca and most necessary during the hot summer months if you intend to keep going into the small hours of the morning! The siesta generally runs from 13.30–17.00 hours, although hypermarkets and department shops remain open, as do many shops in resorts. Mallorcan restaurants don't normally start serving dinner until 20.00 and are at their busiest around 23.00, which is when the discos and clubs too start to fill up, although their special shows do not normally begin until 01.00 or so.

Banks are generally open 08.30–14.30 Mon–Fri and closed on Saturdays. Hours differ in tourist resorts.

PERSONAL COMFORT & SECURITY

Laundry and dry cleaning services are available in hotels. All public establishments have a complaints book or *libro de reclamaciones*.

Public toilets are still not widespread and it is no longer quite so common to wander into a bar merely to use their *servicios* without buying something. Indeed, in Palma, and in other very popular tourist venues, many bars have notices prohibiting just that! You will see signs saying *Aseos reservados para clients* (lavatories reserved for clients only). However, public toilets can be found in hypermarkets, supermarkets, department stores and underground car parks.

Don't leave valuables in your room or car. Don't take your wallet or purse out in the street to buy a carnation from the flower sellers and do beware of timeshare touts with scratch cards indicating that you have won all sorts of goodies if you will just go and take a quick look at some holiday apartments. If you find a ridiculously cheap excursion, treat it with suspicion until you check it out with your travel rep. These frequently end up in a closed environment with hard-sell operators pushing things like blankets.

Lost property should be reported to the local police station, *comisaría*, even if only for insurance purposes. Technically, if found, it should end up at the local town hall. In Palma the number is ⓣ 971 22 59 00

Report lost passports to the Consulate (page 116) and lost credit cards to Mastercard and Visa ⓣ 913 62 62 00; American Express ⓣ 902 37 56 37

POST OFFICES

The Post Office is open from 08.30–14.30 Mon to Fri and Sat from 09.30–13.30. Visitors are recommended to use only the official yellow post boxes when posting mail or postcards, as boxes operated by private companies are not proving to be very reliable. Stamps are also available from any tobacconist or *tabacalera*.

RELIGION

Spain is a Roman Catholic country and visitors are most welcome to attend Mass in local churches. High Mass is celebrated in Palma Cathedral on Sundays and public holidays at 10.30. The Anglican Church is at ⓐ Carrer de Nunyez Balboa 6, Palma ⓣ 971 73 72 79

DIALLING ABROAD

To make an overseas phone call, dial 00 followed by the country code (UK = 44; Ireland = 353), then the local code (minus the initial 0) and the number you want.

TELEPHONES

The Mallorcan Yellow Pages *(Pàgines Grogues)* has a very comprehensive index in English. Its centre pages contain detailed street plans of Palma and other towns.

- **International enquiries** 1825
- **National enquiries** 1818
- **Automatic dialling** 00 + country code + subscriber's number
- **Operator for calls to Europe** 1008

TIME DIFFERENCES

Spain is one hour ahead of GMT and two hours in summertime between the last Sunday in March and the last Sunday in October.

TIPPING

Give a few euros to porters, chambermaids, coach drivers and guides and taxi drivers about 10 per cent of the fare. For tipping in restaurants and bars, see page 97.

WEIGHTS & MEASURES

Spain uses the metric system of kilos and grams but you can always buy two or three apples or half a dozen bananas, for instance. When shopping, you will find that most articles of clothing show British and European sizes

Petrol is sold in litres and you can ask for a full tank – *lleno* – or *diez* (10) euros or *veinte* (20) euros. Distances are in kilometres and metres.

Imperial to metric

1 inch = 2.54 centimetres
1 foot = 30 centimetres
1 mile = 1.6 kilometres
1 ounce = 28 grams
1 pound = 454 grams
1 pint = 0.6 litres
1 gallon = 4.6 litres

Metric to imperial

1 centimetre = 0.4 inches
1 metre = 3 feet, 3 inches
1 kilometre = 0.6 miles
1 gram = 0.04 ounces
1 kilogram = 2.2 pounds
1 litre = 1.8 pints

INDEX

ACKNOWLEDGEMENTS

We would like to thank all the photographers, picture libraries and organisations for the loan of the photographs reproduced in this book, to whom copyright in the photograph belongs:
Brian and Eileen Anderson (pages 5, 16, 21, 31, 52, 66);
Teresa Fisher (pages 75, 90);
Jupiter Images Corporation (pages 109, 125);
Pictures Colour Library Ltd (pages 37, 95, 100, 119);
Thomas Cook Tour Operations Ltd (pages 11, 39, 41, 44, 50, 57, 59, 60, 73, 78, 82, 87, 91, 93, 103, 105);
Geoff Williamson (page 23).

We would also like to thank the following for their contribution to this series:
John Woodcock (map and symbols artwork);
Becky Alexander, Patricia Baker, Sophie Bevan, Judith Chamberlain-Webber, Nicky Gyopari, Stephanie Horner, Krystyna Mayer, Robin Pridy (editorial support);
Christine Engert, Suzie Johanson, Richard Lloyd, Richard Peters, Alistair Plumb, Jane Prior, Barbara Theisen, Ginny Zeal, Barbara Zuñiga (design support).

Send your thoughts to
books@thomascook.com

- **Found a beach bar, peaceful stretch of sand or must-see sight that we don't feature?**
- **Like to tip us off about any information that needs a little updating?**
- **Want to tell us what you love about this handy, little guidebook and more importantly how we can make it even handier?**

Then here's your chance to tell all! Send us ideas, discoveries and recommendations today and then look out for your valuable input in the next edition of this title. And, as an extra 'thank you' from Thomas Cook Publishing, you'll be automatically entered into our exciting monthly prize draw.

Send an email to the above address or write to:
HotSpots Project Editor, Thomas Cook Publishing, PO Box 227, Unit 15/16, Coningsby Road, Peterborough PE3 8SB, UK.